23 DAYS TO ME

Fractal Courage: 23 Days to Me ™
© 2025 Renee King
All rights reserved.

No part of this publication may be reproduced, distributed, or transmitted in any form or by any means, including photocopying, recording, or other electronic or mechanical methods, without the prior written permission of the publisher, except in the case of brief quotations used in reviews, articles, or educational materials permitted by copyright law.

For permission requests, contact the publisher at:
Smarty Pants Publishing ™
A division of Canvas Collective Holdings LLC
   Email: renee@fractalcourage.com
   Website: www.fractalcourage.com

All names, logos, branding marks, and imagery associated with Fractal Courage, The Mastermind Collective, and Canvas Collective are protected trademarks of Canvas Collective Holdings LLC. Unauthorized use or reproduction of these marks, names, or related creative works is strictly prohibited.

This is a work of nonfiction based on the author's personal experiences and reflections. Certain names, identifying details, and events have been changed to protect the privacy of individuals.

Cover design and artwork: © 2025 Renee King
Publisher: Smarty Pants Publishing ™ | Liberty Lake, Washington
Printed in the United States of America
ISBN: **9798275546248**
First Edition: November 17, 2025

23 DAYS TO ME

***Fractal Courage: 23 Days to Me*™**
shows you how to heal, create, and begin again,
one small act of courage at a time.

Finding your Fractals, let's begin...

by Renee King

YOUR GIFT: THE PRACTICE OF BECOMING

A 3-Day Quick Start Guide to Begin Again

Thank you for beginning this journey with **Fractal Courage: 23 Days to Me** ™.

As a gift to you, I've created a 3-day mini sabbatical to help you pause, reflect, and begin again — right where you are.
Inside, you'll find:

- 3 guided reflections to uncover what's holding you back
- 3 micro acts of bravery to interrupt old patterns
- Space to journal, sketch, and start building your new rhythm

This is your quick start to the practice of becoming.

If you're ready to go deeper, **The Fractal Courage Workbook: The Sabbatical for the Soul – A Journey to Becoming** ™ will help you keep going day by day.

Scan Here or Visit
fractalcourage.com/becoming

Scan the QR code above to claim your free **3-Day Quick Start Guide.** You'll receive it by email after checkout confirmation.

The first act of courage is beginning.
The next is continuing.

Join Fractal Courage Movement

Stay Connected. Keep Becoming.

Your journey does not end with the last page of this book. It begins here — in community, in creativity, and in the daily work of becoming.

Visit fractalcourage.com to access:

Events + Workshops
Retreat-style experiences, art and journaling sessions, and live teachings that bring the Fractal Courage framework to life. Perfect for wellness events, women's circles, bookstores, and creative communities.

Interactive Art & Journaling Experiences
Hands-on workshops where you practice the rituals that helped shape Renee's own healing — watercolor, reflective journaling, impermanent art, and pattern interruption practices that restore the nervous system and spark creative renewal.

Speaking Engagements + Book Signings
Invite Renee to speak on creative resilience, reinvention, trauma-aware healing, and the courage to begin again. Live or Virtual Sessions include a talk, Q&A, and signings for in-person events.

Fractal Courage Collective
A guided 90-day coaching experience designed to support your transformation alongside the workbook. Every two weeks, join Renee and guest speakers for a 60-90 minute call where you:
- Deepen your workbook practice
- Build accountability and momentum
- Learn tools for self-regulation, creativity, and pattern interruption
- Connect with others on the same journey

This is not therapy. It is structured support, community insight, and steady encouragement.

Scan Here or Visit fractalcourage.com

You can begin right where you are — and we will walk with you.

THIS BOOK IS DEDICATED TO

The two most important and courageous men in my life, Sam & Ben. Your light in my life has meant more to me than any sunrise.

To my sister Kathy, without you, I would not be the woman I am today. Your warmth, tenacity, and support have meant the world to me.

To the ones who can't see a tomorrow for themselves, may this book and its techniques bring you back into your 'muchness'.

A NOTE FROM THE AUTHOR
RENEE KING

To the One Who is Still Standing,

I have always wanted to be an author, but this isn't the book I ever imagined I would write. Fractal Courage was born out of living a life that broke me open, not one I would have chosen. It came from the quiet work of putting myself back together in pieces, from realizing that courage doesn't always look bold or beautiful. Sometimes it looks like reaching inside to find the fragments of bravery long forgotten and finding a way to bring yourself back into alignment amidst the chaos of life.

The work you are about to begin is rooted in my own dark journey into the light of healing. I did not arrive at these practices through comfort or clarity, but through loss, fear, and deep exhaustion. There were moments I could not see a way forward, times I did not think I could take another breath, let alone rebuild a life that felt fractured beyond repair. I share that not for sympathy, but so you know that I have been where you are standing. Healing often begins when everything familiar falls away and the only way out is through. This work will ask you to look at what has been hidden, to face what you have long ignored, and to sit with what feels uncomfortable. It may feel lonely at times, but I promise you that what waits on the other side of this work is peace, freedom, and a life that finally feels like your own.

During a self-imposed sabbatical, I began to slow down long enough to truly listen. For the first time, to hear my heart, my exhaustion, and the call to begin again. In that stillness, I pulled from years of attending seminars, retreats, and education events throughout my career, gathering the tools and practices that could help me reframe my life. Those lessons became the foundation of the methods I now share in these pages, practical ways to rebuild and reconnect when life feels scattered or uncertain.

I am an interior designer, business coach, and now an author who is still very much on the path. I write and teach about the same principles I am still learning to live out every day. The lessons and steps in these pages are not written from the finish line. They come from what I call the Goodbye Gap, the middle space between what was and what will be. It is the place where healing and becoming happen at the same time, where courage must grow roots before it can bloom.

My two sons are my greatest teachers. They remind me daily that grace, laughter, and connection matter more than getting everything perfect. They are part of the reason I keep showing up to do the work of becoming, again and again.

To you, the reader, thank you for being here. My hope is that Fractal Courage meets you where you are and reminds you that courage still lives within you, even in the smallest pieces. I hope it helps you rediscover your own rhythm of healing and finding beauty in the middle of becoming.

I am not healed, but I am healing. My life is not perfect, but it is mine, and I take pride and joy in the person I am becoming. This book is not a replacement for medication or therapy, but it is a companion for those ready to face hard truths and rebuild from them. On the other side of that choice is the version of you who has been waiting, the one you have always been becoming. They are already within reach, and I cannot wait for you to meet them.

CONTENT

Starting Tomorrow	i
You're Not Broken; You Are Still Becoming	1
The Collapse	7
The Quiet Rebellion	23
Fractals Of Change	37
Reentry + Resurrection	51
The Goodbye Gap - The Framework of Becoming	63
To the Ones Crossing the Gap	79
Continue Your Journey	81
Acknowledgments	83
About the Author	85

STARTING TOMORROW

Starting tomorrow, I begin anew
Starting tomorrow, I will only see the world through the lens of possibility.
Starting tomorrow, I will no longer carry the burdens you placed on my shoulders.

Tomorrow, I will use the strengths I have gained under the weight of your expectations.
To build a new future for myself, one that I create from the remains of my shattered heart.

Starting tomorrow, I will dust off my aching bones and teach them to move again.
The joy of music will fill all my rooms.

Starting tomorrow, I will uncover the joys I savored in my youth.
Filling my days with activities and adventures.
Happy to face every morning's sunrise with a brightness of spirit, I thought
I had lost along the way.

Starting tomorrow, my thoughts will no longer turn to my past.
Tomorrow will be lived as a day to remember.
I will build new memories such that fresh perspectives peak at me from every corner.

The old will be sorted, purged, and set aside.
The new will be brought in only as it pleases me.
My thoughts will no longer entertain hurt and sorrow, regret and sadness.

Starting tomorrow.

- *R. King*

You're Not Broken; You Are Still Becoming

"You're not the same as you were before ... You were much more... muchier... You've lost your muchness."
— *The Mad Hatter (Alice in Wonderland, 2010 film)*

Every story of transformation begins with a single moment of awareness. The instant you realize that the life you are living no longer fits who you are becoming. This introduction invites you to step into that awareness, not as a spectator of my journey, but as the author of your own.

You're not buying a book. You're buying a way back to yourself.

The reason you're here, the reason you picked up this book, the reason you're still breathing in and out, even if just barely? It's because you know. You know that you are meant for more. That you deserve more.

You may not have the words for it yet. But your body knows. It's the part of you that's still showing up, still standing in the quiet. Still whispering, "There has to be another way."

This book is that whisper answered. It's a pattern, a rhythm, a ritual I discovered when I was clawing my way back to the surface of my own life. My hope is that when I fall again, and I will, this book can remind me how to rise. Because it worked, it brought me back to life.

There was a time when I wouldn't leave my bedroom… for weeks, months. My past and my present were continually haunting me, and I couldn't breathe. I'd go from the bed to the bathroom, to maybe the fridge. That was it. Existing, not living, barely functioning. I was trapped in my own life, suffocating inside walls I had built and didn't know how to tear down. In some way, I knew that I had lost myself and lacked the drive to find myself again. It was as though I had forgotten how to participate in daily life. As if isolation would save me from myself.

But here's what I didn't see, even then, that version of me wasn't asking for help. I didn't even know I needed it yet. I was still breaking, but I hadn't yet realized how sick I was. I didn't know that numbness was a symptom. That isolation was a red flag. That hiding was a sign of something deeper.

The real turning point wasn't crawling out of bed. It was recognizing that I needed to. It was when I finally admitted that what I was living wasn't life, it was survival. Living the way I was, I wasn't really alive, and my children needed me to show them that it's possible not just to survive, but to thrive. Something I also needed to prove to myself.

That's when I stepped into triage. And here's what no one tells you: Getting to triage isn't the breakthrough; it's the beginning. The path to healing is long, and it starts with the moment you stop pretending you are fine. Triage is the quiet recognition that survival is not the same as living. It is the point where you finally see the wounds you have ignored, where you begin to sort what can be saved from what must be released. It's not heroic or cinematic; it's raw, humbling work. You face yourself in the harsh light of truth and realize that you cannot go back to who you were, but you can begin again from where you are.

And the truth - the one that wrecked me and saved me all at once - is this: No one is coming to save you. It was the loneliest moment of my life, and yet it was somehow the most empowering.

When you stop waiting for someone else to fix what is broken, you begin to understand that the power to change has been within you all along. Help may arrive through friends, therapy, or faith, but it can only meet you where you are willing to begin. Healing is not about isolation; it is about ownership. Others can guide, hold space, and remind you of your strength, but only you can take the steps. That is where transformation begins, not in being saved, but in choosing - every single day - to save yourself. The recognition that our thoughts, choices, and actions are ours alone. We get to decide to direct, control, and intervene on our journey to self-discovery.

For the first time, I realized that if I wasn't steering the ship... then who was?

No one! And that was the problem. That's how I got here - waiting. Hoping someone else would make the move. Take control, save me, but they didn't. And they weren't going to, so I did. That moment of terrifying clarity became the spark. In the absence of someone to rescue me, I became the one I had been waiting for. Not my therapist. Not my partner. Not my family. Not my best friend.

And here's where you come in, because at some point, you'll have to become the one you've been waiting for, too. Not your therapist. Not your partner. Not your family. Not your best friend.

Only you can do the real work. Only you can decide that you are done living inside the tornado, the daily erosion of self, the chaos you allow to control you. Only you can pull yourself out of the spinning, out of the survival, out of the story you tell yourself that this is all you get, all you deserve.

The first step on the journey to your true self begins now. Not in some perfect moment of clarity, but here, in the middle of the mess. You have all the tools within you; it's time to step into your power.

This book and the companion workbook will guide you. You'll find tools. You'll find rituals. You'll learn to find the stillness you need to rest, and the space you need to release what's been held too long.

 "Art washes away from the soul the dust of everyday life." - Pablo Picasso

You'll also be invited to tap into your creative spirit, the part of you that knows how to express without permission. You don't need to be "an artist." You don't need to be perfect or trained or talented. You just need to be willing.

Creative expression has a way of slipping past the guards we post at the door of our own minds and speaking straight to the wounds that words can't reach. It can remind us that beauty can be made from mess, and that not everything we create has to last forever to matter.

In these pages, you'll find small, simple ways to create, not for performance, but for permission. Permission to step into yourself, that person you were always meant to be. Later, I'll tell you about a nightly practice that became my lifeline, teaching me the art of letting go and starting again. For now, just know this: your creativity might be the bridge between who you've been and who you're becoming.

Let it take any form it needs to. Journal your truth, paint your exhaustion, walk until your mind quiets. Doodle your grief. Stitch your hope. Let the act itself be enough. Healing begins when you stop trying to make art good and start letting it make you whole.

This is about creating space to feel again, not to produce or perfect, but to simply exist within your own becoming. To return to yourself in motion, without judgment or outcome. Each act becomes a quiet reminder that feeling is not failure; it is proof that you are still here, still capable of beauty, still becoming.

Come back to them again and again. Give yourself time. Give yourself grace. The mountain you face to get back to yourself is steep. Most people don't make the climb. But you can!

I wanted to build something beautiful this time. So I had to show up, not for anyone else, for me. I began to imagine what the life I wanted looked like, felt like. In the months ahead, I would discover something I now call Fractal Courage.

It began with 23 days alone; a self-imposed sabbatical in which I unraveled, reimagined, and rebuilt my life one tiny act at a time. But we'll get to that later. In silence, I found not emptiness but truth. When the noise fell away, what remained was the quiet voice that had been waiting to guide me home.

Recovery isn't just about getting out of pain. It's about re-learning how to treat your wounds. You wouldn't expect someone recovering from surgery to run a marathon the next day. You'd tell them to rest. To nourish themselves. To eat, sleep, breathe.

So why do we expect ourselves to recover from trauma, loss, change, heartbreak, or depression, and immediately return to the same pace and chaos that hurt us? You've just come from war. Your body, your mind, your soul;

they need recovery time.

For me, stepping out of my toxic marriage and the life I had built was like stepping out of a tornado. I thought chaos was normal. Spinning was normal. Walls crumbling around me? That was just Tuesday. But when I finally stepped out, I saw the storm for what it really was. And then came the void. Because when you leave the tornado, you don't just feel peace. You feel the absence, the vacuum where the chaos used to live. It's disorienting. But it's also an invitation.

Your job now is to fill that space with the things that bring you back to yourself. With your muchness. That muchness; the thing you've given away to everyone else now belongs to you. All that love you've poured into others? It's time to turn it inward.

You are more than what you've been through. You are more than your pain. You are more than your silence. And if you've forgotten that this book is here to help you remember.

This book is not a manual for escape; it is a mirror for return. Each chapter offers a reflection of what happens when we stop running from our pain and start listening to it. Inside these pages, you will not find quick fixes. You will find a rhythm. A fractal pattern of small acts, repeated until courage becomes your new way of being.

You haven't lost your muchness. You're just learning how to hold it again.

Fractal Courage In Motion

I wrote this book as a companion, not a manual. You don't have to fix or force anything here. You only have to arrive exactly as you are and let the words meet you where you've been hiding.

You don't have to rush or take notes. This book was written to be experienced, not finished. Along the way, you'll see small callouts marked **Fractal Reflection, Fractal Courage In Motion: Fractal Act, and Fractal Practice.** These aren't assignments. They're invitations.

Fractal Reflections are moments of pause and perspective - where awareness becomes insight. They are your checkpoints along the journey, inviting you to look inward and notice what is shifting. Reflection turns experience into wisdom. These reflections are how you recognize your growth, name your patterns, and decide how to begin again. They're not about judgment; they're about seeing yourself with compassion and clarity.

A **Fractal Act** is a small, visible movement - something you can do right now to remind yourself you are still becoming. It might be as simple as taking one slow breath, writing one honest line, or letting the sunlight find your face.

A **Fractal Practice** is the space that follows - the pause, the noticing, the reflection that turns movement into meaning. It might be journaling what you felt, sketching, painting, or sitting in quiet until the body softens.

Together, these acts and practices form a rhythm... notice, do, reflect, repeat.

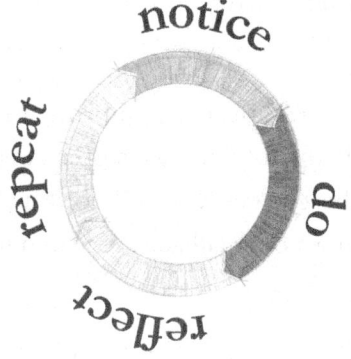

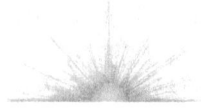

 Collapse

"Fear does not prevent death. It prevents life."
— Naguib Mahfouz

The Weight Of Holding It All

Every collapse begins with a build-up. Slowly, over time, the weight of our burdens settles on us. It's subtle at first, so easy to miss, each new worry, obligation, or wound becoming another stone in the pack we carry. We tell ourselves it's fine. We can handle it. Until one day, the weight is untenable, and we can no longer remember how it got so heavy.

This chapter marks the moment the walls began to close in, the point when I knew the life I had been living was no longer survivable. My collapse was not sudden. It was a quiet, relentless erosion, years in the making. And when it finally came, it stripped away everything familiar. Here, I will take you into that season of agoraphobia, depression, and disconnection, not to dwell in the darkness, but to show you the truth I learned: the only way out is through.

My whole life, I prided myself on being a high performer. I got good grades, graduated with honors, and knocked out every life goal I set for myself. I was the first in my family to get a college degree. I was a faithful wife, a mother to 2 sons, and owned my own award-winning design firm with a small team of employees and projects spanning the US and Canada. From the outside, I am sure our family and my life looked successful and fulfilled. If I set my sights on something, I generally achieved it. I was constantly on the move, running to that next goalpost.

When The Cracks Begin to Show

Trigger Warning: This chapter includes references to trauma, abuse, depression, and suicidal ideation. Reader discretion is advised. Take breaks as needed and seek support if you experience emotional distress.

The reality of my daily life couldn't have been farther from that perception of truth. I was performing. I was performing in every aspect of my life. Trying to fill a role, whether wife, mother, or business owner, I did what I needed to do to get to the end of every day. But inside, that was a different story. I was broken, empty. Every day was painful. I lived in fear, in a lie I taught myself, that I would come up short for those I loved, that I was not enough.

I volunteered within my design community and juggled my work schedule with childcare, always trying to make it all fit. My then-husband worked swing shifts on weekends, and we rarely found time for family activities together. I often felt like a single mother, carrying the financial strain of running a business, handling the household chores, overseeing homework, cooking meals, rearing our two rambunctious sons, all of it landing squarely on my shoulders. I was burning the candle at both ends for everyone but myself. Somewhere in the chaos, I forgot about me. My waking thoughts were consumed with "what's next?" until overwhelm became not just a feeling, but my default state of being.

My childhood appeared picture-perfect—school awards, church involvement, and family photos that spoke of harmony. Behind that facade was a lesson in survival. I learned that love had to be earned, that silence was safer than truth, and that approval was a moving target. Those early lessons became the blueprint for every unhealthy relationship that followed.

In public, we were flawless. At church and family gatherings, we played the part of a picture-perfect family. My mother was a master illusionist, rewriting truth with practiced ease. I learned to perform, to smile on cue, and to keep the secrets that held our image together. That performance became my survival. It taught me that love meant earning approval and that affection always came with a price. It wasn't silence that kept me safe; it was adaptation. I learned early that survival meant becoming whatever version of myself the moment required. It was a performance so convincing, I forgot it wasn't real.

That early conditioning followed me into adulthood. I did not recognize it then, but the man I later married carried the same traits I had been trained to navigate since childhood. The same charm that could flip to cruelty, the same shifting of truth, the same rewriting of reality until I questioned my own. I mistook familiarity for safety. I confused chaos with passion, and control with love. Because that was the language I had been taught to understand.

I had suffered from depression for as long as I can remember, even as a child; the weight of existing sometimes felt unbearable. At eight or nine, I tried to choke myself, though I did not understand why. By sixteen, I had to concentrate hard when driving to stop myself from veering into oncoming traffic. I had no idea that these dark thoughts were not weakness but symptoms, the result of years of emotional neglect and abuse that had quietly convinced me I had no worth. I truly believed the world would be better off without me.

Throughout my teens and into adulthood, I cycled in and out of therapy, on and off medications, searching for something that could quiet the noise inside my head. Nothing seemed to reach the root. So I did what so many of us do when we are drowning. I stayed busy. I filled every waking hour with distraction, work, achievement, helping others, anything to avoid being alone with myself. And slowly, almost imperceptibly, the depression began to dictate the rhythm of my days. It became the silent pulse underneath everything, shaping how I worked, loved, and lived.

Fractal Reflection:

What are you carrying that no one sees?

What would happen if you set one stone down, just for today?

The Breaking Point

The fall before the Pandemic, I was in a serious car crash, and that began my final unraveling. It started slowly, the way storms roll in without warning. A creeping gray that dulled the edges of my days. Depression and agoraphobia moved in quietly until they were all I knew. I had lost my sense of self long before I realized it was gone.

As a result of the car crash, I suffered a traumatic brain injury, one that left me unable to recall words, speak clearly, with a deafening ringing in my ears, and sensitivity to light and motion. In the days and months that followed, I began to retreat entirely to my bedroom and my bed. I began to operate my business (what little was left) from bed. I didn't have it in me to even care for myself. Brushing my teeth seemed like an impossible feat, leaving my bedroom became the scariest thing I could do with my day.

As I struggled to keep my business afloat and stay financially stable, the world was also shutting down as the realities of the worldwide pandemic became part of our daily existence. Layering a new kind of uncertainty and isolation onto an already fragile foundation. Being unable to run my business became a quick reality, and within months, I had shut down my studio and let my employees go. The embarrassment of that perceived failure began to seep into my bones.

It became easy to hide behind the excuse that the Pandemic provided. I was isolated because I had to be, not because I was hiding from my life.

I started bowing out of activities I used to find relaxing and retreated from my friends and family. I had no time for myself. I was constantly worrying about dropping the ball and letting people down. Isolation crept in, and the realities of shouldering the load of my family and my business were quickly becoming too much for me to face every day. I began to miss meetings, avoid phone calls, and emails. I would delay going into the office. Turned to sleep to ease the ache and weight of the daily demands of my schedule. Amid this busy life, I lost myself. I began to be numb to my surroundings. And the slow retreat inward began deepening, without my notice, one day at a time.

It got to the point where I would turn off my camera for video calls with client meetings. I retreated so far into myself that it felt like I needed to remove an elephant from my chest just to go through the motions. I still traveled for work. For those few trips, I had to hype myself up to pretend to be normal. I would go to meetings, smile, present my concepts, and do my best to appear fine. All the while, I was counting the minutes until I could retreat to my hotel room. Inside, I felt like my clients and colleagues would realize at any moment I was falling apart.

I felt as though part of me was screaming in some small corner of my brain, crying for help. It was as though I had a tell-tale heart like an Edgar Allen Poe story building inside me, and at any moment, everyone around me would witness my unraveling. I was sure they could sense it, positive that at any moment I would be committed.

At home, my light often felt too bright. I learned to dim it, to soften my success so it would not unsettle the fragile balance between my husband and I. Each achievement that should have felt like joy instead felt like something to manage, something to downplay. I stopped celebrating milestones altogether. Somewhere along the way, I mistook keeping the peace for love. But even as I built a career that looked like success from the outside, I felt hollow inside. I had everything I was supposed to want: career, home, family, and yet, I could not feel any of it.

The silence I kept eventually became its own kind of prison. I had built a life that looked beautiful on paper, but it was one I could no longer live inside. Each time I silenced myself to keep the peace, I drifted a little farther from who I was. I mistook control for stability, achievement for worth, and quiet for safety. But inside, the walls were closing in. **Success without self-worth is a slow suffocation, an elegant kind of collapse that no one else can see until it is too late.** And when it finally broke, it didn't sound like an explosion. It was a quiet shattering, the kind that only the soul can hear.

The Quiet Unraveling

I had a few pivotal experiences over the coming years that began to open my eyes to the reality of how sick I had become. How far I had fallen. I was a shell; my children would beg me to get help. But they seemed so far away from me. I couldn't hear their voices. I would see them standing next to me or at the door to my bedroom, and yet, I couldn't hear them. As if they stood on a far-off shore and I could only perceive the tenor of their voice, not the words they were speaking. A foreign language to my ears.

Years of putting my husband's needs ahead of everyone else's took a toll I could no longer ignore. Somewhere along the way, I began to see how that imbalance had shaped my children, too. In trying to keep the peace, I had allowed harm to ripple through our home. My silence became complicity. My efforts to appease him meant that I often agreed when I didn't believe, enforced rules I didn't support, and stood by when I should have protected. Supporting my children was seen as disloyalty, and so I learned to choose survival over truth.

I had slowly wrapped myself around managing my husband, his moods, his tempers, his expectations, until there was little space left for anything else. Every decision, every reaction, every breath became a calculation of what might keep the day from exploding. The cost of that choice is something I still reckon with: the quiet grief of realizing that in shielding my family from one kind of chaos, I had created another.

My mother and my husband were both expert reality-altering engineers. Perfect at redirection and misdirection. I learned to live in their world of false reality. Living with narcissists became a game, where rules were ever shifting like sand on the shore. Learning to navigate the web, they would weave, one, they would create and destroy on a whim. This led me to live in their wonderland. Accepting their lies as truth and my truth as a lie. Self-denial, self-isolation, self-minimizing, where all tools I learned to wield daily.

The first fundamental moment that changed me forever came as I was healing from the crash. As my brain began to right itself, I was flooded with memories from my childhood, long-forgotten images that I had tucked so far into the shadows of myself that I didn't even know they were there, waiting.

One morning, as I was waking up, a scent drifted through the room and pulled me back to an afternoon in my childhood bedroom. A memory surfaced, sharp, uninvited, undeniable. I remembered the moment when trust was broken - when something sacred was taken before I had words to understand it. I recalled the weight of betrayal, the confusion, the fear, and the silence that followed. My body remembered before my mind caught up. I lay there frozen, realizing for the first time how early pain had taken root and shaped every corner of my life.

Yet that memory, painful as it was, became the fracture that let the light in. I began to see the lineage of sorrow that ran through the women in my family: the suppression, the denial, the desperate need to appear fine. My mother's cruelty was born of her own unhealed wounds, passed down like an inheritance of survival. But I knew then that it would end with me. I would not pass that silence on to my children.

That was the moment I began to live, not perfectly, not all at once, but consciously. It was the first step in breaking free from the inheritance of suffering, the quiet rebellion to end what had been passed down for generations.

My mother's family carried the weight of unspoken trauma. My grandfather had taken his own life years before I was born, and that single act rippled through generations in ways no one ever named. The women in our family learned to survive by suppressing pain, performing strength, and passing on silence as inheritance. Broken daughters raising broken children, each doing the best they could with the tools they were given, yet never truly healing, only coping. Looking back, I believe this is where my mother's narcissism was born. It wasn't a choice, but a defense, a way to armor herself against pain so unbearable it had nowhere else to go.

During this time, one of my maternal aunts was nearing the end of her life. I spent a night with her the week she passed, sitting beside her hospital bed and holding her soft, trembling hand. The air in the room felt heavy with both sorrow and unfinished stories. I was overwhelmed by grief for her pain, gratitude for the brief closeness we shared, and a profound sadness for the deep-rooted suffering she carried her whole life.

She drifted in and out of consciousness, her voice rising in fragile bursts of anguish. At times, it did not sound entirely human, more like the cry of a soul desperate to be free. She pleaded for time: time to make things right with her family, to ask forgiveness, to mend what had been broken. It was a lament that seemed to echo through generations, a haunting mix of regret and longing.

Watching her struggle to let go was surreal, like witnessing the spirit itself wrestle with the weight of unhealed wounds. In that moment, I saw not just her pain, but the pain of all the women before us, each carrying burdens that were never truly theirs to bear. It was a sobering truth that shook me to my core. I made a silent vow that night: I would not wait until my final breath to make things right. I would face my truth now, while I still had time to live it.

That night with my aunt stayed with me. Her cries for more time echoed long after she was gone, haunting me in the quiet moments when I was alone with my thoughts. I began to see how pain unspoken becomes a legacy, passed from mother to daughter, generation to generation, until someone decides to stop carrying it. But breaking that cycle comes at a cost. When you finally decide to face what others buried, you awaken everything they refused to feel. The grief, the rage, and the exhaustion all rise to the surface at once. I thought I could handle it. I thought awareness alone was enough. But soon the weight of everything I had uncovered began to pull me under. That was the beginning of my descent, the moment I found myself standing at the edge of the abyss.

Those moments changed me, though I did not yet understand how deeply. It would be years before I found the strength to take control, to steer my life instead of being carried by its current.

The Edge Of The Abyss

Self-Care Note: If this section stirs painful memories, pause and breathe. Reach for a supportive friend or professional.

In the midst of all of these revelations, we moved out of state for my ex-husband's job. This only further added to my sense of isolation and codependency. I continued to unravel until one fateful afternoon when I found myself at a crossroads. As a high performer, I was traditionally a person who had plans. I had plans for my plans. If path A wasn't viable, I had path B and then back-up plans for those plans. I was constantly looking to a future version of my life; for myself, my family, my children.

I had retreated so far from who I was that most days I lay in bed, sobbing. That morning, when I woke, I realized I had no plans. For the first time in my life, I couldn't see a tomorrow for myself. I couldn't see a path to the next moment, let alone the coming days, weeks, or years.

There was a firearm in the house. In my state of mind, it became a plan. I told myself that leaving might spare my family the burden of my failures. That, in some distorted way, I would be rescuing them from me. I took it with me into the bathroom and posted a note on the door: Do not enter. Call the police.

As the darkness surrounded me and shrouded my sight from the next moment, I contemplated my end, and for a brief moment, I felt relief. The bathroom floor became both sanctuary and reckoning. It was where I stopped running from myself. That cold tile caught every piece of me that had been breaking for years. The mother, the wife, the woman who forgot she mattered. There, I whispered the first honest words I had said in years: I cannot do this anymore.

My dog Lily began to scratch at the bathroom door and bark and cry as if she knew what I was planning. Somehow, her barking woke me up. What was I thinking?!? I was choosing death over learning to live again… I knew better; I had seen the generational devastation suicide could have on a family firsthand. This was the best I could do for my family? Really?!?

When I opened that bathroom door and stepped into the hallway, it was as if I could see the sun, feel its warmth, as if I hadn't seen it in years. The light filled my soul with a glimpse of what a new beginning might look like. I owed it to my children and to myself to find a different path to tomorrow.

I was filled at once with both fear and longing, a longing to get back to myself. To find a path back to the me I was, the me I had yet to become. Not only for my sons but most importantly for myself. A yearning to get back to my younger self that was fearless, that was eager and burning to experience all that life had to offer. To sit again under a sky full of stars and stare in wonder at the beauty around me.

A fear that, to my surprise, no longer filled me with dread or terror. Instead, it shifted, morphed, into something almost electric. An anticipation of who I could become, even though I had no map, no clear instructions, no step-by-step plan. All I knew was that it had to start now. Suddenly, there was no going back.

The First Breath Of Becoming

It was the "burn the ships" moment I'd read about when leaders landed on foreign shores and set fire to their own vessels so there could be no retreat. The only direction was forward. I realized I had to do the same. I couldn't keep one foot in the wreckage of the life I was leaving and expect to fully step into what was next. I had to let the flames consume the safety nets, the backup plans, the false comforts.

Fractal Courage In Motion

Fractal Act: The First Breath Back

In collapse, the body becomes the last refuge. Naming your breath and your existence brings you back to your center. Sit where you are. Don't change your posture or try to improve your breathing, just notice it. Place your hand lightly on your chest or stomach and feel the rise and fall.

Whisper to yourself, "I'm still here." That's all you have to do. One breath noticed is one thread of life reclaimed.

Fractal Practice: Life's Connection

Find a small notebook, a scrap of paper, or the notes app on your phone. Write down one thing, just one, that still connects you to life. It might be the sound of a loved one's voice, the smell of rain, the warmth of a blanket, or the feel of sunlight through a window.

Tomorrow, write one more. Over time, you'll gather proof that even in isolation, life was still reaching for you.

In that moment, my past stopped being a place I could return to. The only way forward was through, toward a self I had yet to meet, but was already waiting for me on the other side of fear. I knew I had to cut ties with the version of me who waited for rescue. The fear that had once kept me paralyzed began to shift into a strange kind of exhilaration. I didn't yet know who I could become, but I knew the only way to meet her was to keep moving toward the unknown. The life I had been living was gone. What came next would have to be built from scratch.

But first, I had to strip away the illusions I'd been living under. I had to take off the glasses that painted my life in colors that weren't real, the lenses that let me pretend I was fine when, in truth, I was crumbling. That false reality had been my survival mechanism, but it had also kept me blind to just how sick, depleted, and disconnected I had become. Facing the truth meant looking at every part of my life without flinching: my marriage, my health, my finances, my emotional state, my friendships, my identity. It meant standing in the wreckage without rushing to sweep it up, letting myself see the mess in its full, unfiltered reality.

It was terrifying. And it was freeing. Because once I could see where I really was, I could finally start to chart a way out. The journey ahead wasn't going to be about fixing everything at once; it would be about learning to face each broken piece, one at a time, and finding the courage to repair what I could and let go of what no longer served me or deserved my time.

Fractal Reflection:

What truth in your life have you been afraid to name? Write it down. Speak it, even if only to yourself.

Naming is the first act of release — a promise to stop carrying what no longer belongs to you.

It was as if the fog I had lived in for years had finally burned off. The world snapped into sharp, undeniable focus, every detail, every truth, suddenly visible. For the first time in a long time, I could truly see. And the first step was to look at my life exactly as it was, in full color, without filter, excuse, or condition.

Part of learning how to show up for myself began when I decided to live the life I had only allowed myself to imagine. I had to learn what that looked like and how to get there the hard way. For years, I had been on autopilot, moving through my days with the dull weight of responsibility pressing down, but without a clear sense of my own place in the world. I had been surviving, alive but not living. I didn't notice how far I'd drifted from myself until the silence after the storm made it impossible to ignore.

There's a strange kind of terror that comes when you realize no one is coming to fix this for you, but there's also a thrilling kind of freedom. That freedom is raw, almost wild, and it whispers the truth: if no one is coming, then you are free to decide what comes next. You are the creator of your destination.

In the days and weeks that followed, I began to piece together a plan, a way to come back to life. To see my world exactly as it was, without distortion or excuse, and then to carve a new path into the unknown. I would have to teach myself, step by step, what it meant to truly stand in my own corner. And I knew that as I learned to live for myself, I was also showing my sons what it looks like to rise. To become a truer, stronger version of who I was, and to turn recovery into something more than survival. To turn it into triumph.

Healing was not a single awakening but a collection of small, stubborn choices. To wake up. To eat. To walk outside. Each act was a protest against the lie that I was beyond repair.

I decided that, though this was my path and my challenge, I couldn't walk it alone. I needed someone to help me build the framework for what this new life could look like, and to imagine what it might feel like if I let go of everything holding me back. I sought therapy and took that first step on my thousand-mile journey back to myself.

> **Fractal Reflection:**
>
> Write one sentence beginning with: *Today, I choose to see myself as...*

Allow honesty, not perfection.

In my professional career, I attended hundreds of hours of personal and professional development seminars. My immediate thought was that to see my life clearly, I had to get substantial time away from my daily life and my husband. So I began to build a personal retreat. Pulling lessons from those hours of instruction, I knew I had to set clear expectations and outcomes. What was I wanting to accomplish? That perfect day in the life of my future self? What would it take to get there? What do I need right now to help me take that first step into becoming me again?

I knew immediately that I needed rest! Bone deep, thought stirring, open my brain, rest. I needed to retreat from my daily reality. I needed new energy to carry me into that new future. One of my earliest realizations was that, to truly see where I stood, I had to remove the noise of daily life. I needed a safe place to think, to hear my own voice again, to strip away the chaos. That's when I created a plan to **Rest, Retreat, and Recharge.**

Since my work was fully remote and all I needed was an internet connection, I searched for a place where I could spend 30 days alone, rebuilding from the inside out. The best I could find was a quiet spot in the mountains, available for exactly 23 days. It felt almost symbolic: 2023, the year of the **"23 Days to Me"**.

Knowing I would need structure to avoid falling into my old habit of living from my bed, I created a framework for what I envisioned success might feel like:

Week 1: Find Out What I'm Facing
Week 2: Discover What I Love
Week 3: Learn To Love Where I Am

This was the first time in my life I began showing up for myself, not in one grand gesture, but in small, fractal acts that added up to courage. This, I thought, was the opening act of showing up for myself.

I didn't know what healing looked like, but I knew what dying felt like. So I chose the unknown.

Fractal Courage In Motion

Fractal Act: The Steady Return

A grounding exercise to help anchor the nervous system and affirm survival without rushing to healing:

Find a quiet space and sit comfortably. Feel your feet against the ground or the weight of your body on the chair. Place one hand over your heart and one on your stomach. Inhale slowly, counting to four. As you exhale, imagine letting go of everything that is no longer yours to carry — the stories, the expectations, the survival strategies that once kept you safe. Repeat three times.

If emotions rise, let them. That's what returning feels like: messy, human, alive.

Fractal Practice: The First Light

Transform recognition into repetition, the start of a new pattern. When you wake tomorrow, before reaching for your phone or replaying the day ahead, take one conscious breath. Whisper, "This is what beginning feels like." In your journal or notes app, write one sentence that begins with:

"Today, I will honor my becoming by…"

The sentence can be simple, by resting, by saying no, by taking a walk, by telling the truth. End your entry by writing: "I am learning to live again."

The Quiet Rebellion

"Courage isn't one moment. It's a million tiny acts."
– R. King

The Silence I Chose

There's something about growing up under the weight of other people's damage that changes the way you see the world. From my parents, I learned early how to survive in an environment where love was conditional, and reality could be rewritten overnight. I learned to adapt, to shape-shift, to keep the peace by creating a version of the truth that was easier to live with.

From my marriage, I learned how easily I could disappear inside someone else's needs, how quickly I could lose myself in the quiet drip of criticism, control, and contempt. In both places, I became an expert at running from reality, at telling myself a story that kept me functioning but never truly free.

My 23-day sabbatical didn't look like a wellness retreat. There were no yoga mats or green juices. It looked like silence. I silenced the digital world; phone off, television dark, every feed closed, until only music and my own breath remained. I shut down the outside world so I could finally hear my own voice. It had been buried under years of noise, obligation, abuse, redirection, and the expectations of everyone but me. I didn't retreat to escape my life. I retreated to meet it head-on.

I structured those twenty-three days around a living rhythm: Rest to restore, Retreat to reflect, and Recharge to rise again. Each phase was not a checklist but a return to self. First to face what was real, then to rediscover joy, and finally to practice loving where I already stood. To achieve these three outcomes, I needed a framework to work from. One of the self-destructive tools I got a lot of use out of was dissociation, focusing on the noise and chaos to drown out my inner voice. To heal, I needed quiet, the kind that forces you to sit in the discomfort you've been avoiding.

Silence was dangerous back then, because in silence, the truth could get too loud. So I learned to fill my days with busyness, noise, and distraction. If I kept moving, I wouldn't see the cracks. If you've ever lived like that, you know, your body forgets what stillness feels like, and your mind forgets how to listen to itself. Only later did I learn that silence could hold me, not haunt me.

"Rest. Retreat. Recharge." That became my rhythm. It wasn't indulgent. It was medicine. Rest taught me to stop performing. Retreat showed me the beauty of solitude. Recharge reminded me that stillness could be strength. I began splitting my day into quarters: morning, noon, midday, and evening. If I failed one part, I didn't abandon the day. I started the next quarter fresh. I began to dampen my inner critic and learn to let go, to loosen my grip and my desire to control.

I asked my family not to call or text me during this time unless it was urgent. This wasn't about being selfish or shutting people out. It was about finally centering myself, finding my own gravity after years of orbiting around everyone else's needs. I needed to step out of the constant pull of obligation and into a place where I could hear my own heartbeat again. This was my chance to build a way out of the darkness I had allowed to consume me, brick by brick, breath by breath.

But here, in the quiet I had chosen for myself within my sabbatical, there was nowhere to run. The stories I'd used to survive began to unravel, leaving behind the raw edges of what was real. While that was terrifying, it was also the beginning of something new, the choice to see my life as it really was, not as I'd been told it should be.

Making Space for Truth – The Framework

This was not about perfection. It was about pattern interruption. Rewiring my relationship to time, energy, and self-worth. No one was coming to save me, and no one was watching. Which meant I got to decide what my healing looked like.

Each day, I allowed myself to wake naturally. No alarms, no panic about being "on time". Just the quiet gift of waking when my mind and body were ready. Without the pressure, I found I woke naturally around 8 or 9 a.m., and even that felt like a small victory. A lifetime of insomnia had often led me to little sleep or late morning wake-up times. As I had spent years in self-imposed isolation in my bed, I knew I would have to be intentional about staying up and engaged.

My Daily Framework:

Step 1: Make breakfast, Step 2: Actually eat it (I used to eat at my desk and work through lunch or breakfast, which inevitably meant I would forget the whole eating part)Step 3: Clean up and brush my teeth. Get dressed for the day and keep my shoes on so I wouldn't slide back under the covers.

Noon and midday hours were for the essentials: a few work tasks, sorting bills, organizing mail, and taking stock of my finances. This was my way of "cleaning out the closets" of my life. Some afternoons, I'd go for nature walks or sit on the porch, letting the breeze, the scent of pine, and the sounds of birds remind me I was part of a living, breathing world.

Evenings were for making dinner, tidying up, and then my healing rituals: journaling, painting, and reading. I didn't treat these as simple hobbies; they were medicine for my mind and soul.

Once I removed all distractions, when the quiet came, it wasn't instantly peaceful. At first, it was uncomfortable. I didn't know what to do without the chaos, and I had to fight the urge to fill the space with scrolling, with background noise, with "just one more task."

As I began the journey to Find out what I was Facing, I quickly learned that silence offers no hiding place. It reflects you back to yourself like a room of mirrors, showing not punishment but possibility. Without distractions, every reflection shows a piece of yourself you have avoided, truths you buried so deep you almost forgot they existed. The quiet becomes both your witness and your teacher.

It's the moment when you come face-to-face with the raw, unedited version of you. The one that exists beneath the roles, the noise, and the armor. Entering that mirrored room feels dangerous because you don't know what you'll find. You begin to see yourself clearly, to meet every hidden part of your story, and to understand that healing starts with the courage to keep looking. There is strength in seeing and accepting every version of yourself. To begin to see where healing can start. If you stay long enough, keep looking, and refuse to turn away, you emerge changed. Stripped of illusion, steadier, and somehow more whole.

That courage doesn't always come in grand gestures. It comes in micro-acts: sitting in silence and allowing your thoughts to wander, finishing a page of a book before moving on, taking a deep breath and just… be.

Fractal Reflection:

When was the last time you truly heard your own voice beneath the noise of others' expectations?

What stories have you been performing to keep the peace, and what truth is waiting beneath the act?

The Art That Saved Me

Every night, I committed to creating one painting, not as an artist seeking perfection, but as a human being searching for truth. I had always been in love with art; creativity had been woven into me since childhood. In this chapter of my life, art took on an entirely different role. I wasn't trying to produce something beautiful for the world to admire. I was trying to make sense of my own existence, to give shape and color to feelings I couldn't always name.

I chose watercolors for their unpredictability, the way the pigment blooms and runs like a living thing. My canvas was always the same: a simple 12x12 square, waiting for me at the end of each day. I would let the brush move however it wanted, sometimes slow and deliberate, sometimes wild and unrestrained, until an image, a pattern, or simply a feeling began to emerge. Some nights I tried to mirror an image I had in mind; other nights, I chose colors just for the way they spoke to me; and sometimes I let instinct lead entirely, painting whatever felt right in the moment.

I would end the evening with journaling, pouring out what the day had carried: the quiet victories, the lingering pain, the questions without answers. Free writing was foreign to me, so I set a timer. As the days went on, journaling became easier. Some nights, I set a goal just to write whatever came without thought, expectation, or judgment. Some nights, I would create intentional exercises, task myself to write a poem or a memory that stirred me. Sometimes, journaling time was spent re-reading what I had written the previous night.

I named each day's painting from words or phrases pulled from my journaling that night. Names like: 'Chaos', 'More to Give', 'Here, if Nowhere Else'.

The next morning, I would photograph the piece as a way of honoring it, and then I would wash it away. The paint would swirl down the drain, leaving behind only faint traces of color. That night, I would paint over the same surface, layering new life on the remnants of the old. It reminded me of the Tibetan monks' intricate sand mandalas, hours of careful creation, then a deliberate act of destruction to honor impermanence.

In that ritual, I learned to release. I learned that nothing, no feeling, no memory, no moment, has to be permanent for it to matter. Some nights the process felt like therapy; other nights, like prayer, and a few nights it felt like torture. Over time, I began to notice how each layer of color, no matter how chaotic, left a shadow behind, quietly influencing what came next. It was the perfect metaphor for my own healing: not erasing the past, but integrating it into something new.

This was not about making art. This was about rebuilding my inner world one brushstroke at a time, accepting that the process was messy and imperfect, and that was the point. It was here, in this quiet, repetitive practice, that I

Fractal Courage In Motion

Fractal Act: The Doing

Choose one daily act that interrupts an old habit: pause before reacting, breathe before responding, or sit in silence before deciding. These micro-moments are acts of rebellion toward peace.

Fractal Practice: The Becoming

Find a place today to sit in silence for five minutes, let your thoughts wander, and observe where your mind takes you. Write down your impressions. Try to go for ten minutes tomorrow.

Each night, write one sentence starting with 'I allowed myself to…'. This reflection cements self-permission and awareness, the essence of re-patterning.

began to reclaim pieces of myself I thought were lost forever. Each small act of awareness echoing the last until transformation felt inevitable.

It became a ritual of release. Washing away what I had done the night before taught me that not everything needed to be preserved to have meaning, and that beauty could live in the temporary. This was never about producing something for others to see. This was about permitting myself to process, to feel, and to begin again. In those nightly sessions, I learned to let go, to loosen my grip on perfection and control. To accept imperfection, and to trust that even what was washed away helped shape what came next.

This chapter of my life wasn't loud. It wasn't dramatic; it was quiet. But it was rebellion all the same, rebellion against the life that had been slowly draining me, and the first step toward creating one worth living.

I was breaking the old agreement I'd made with the world, that my worth was tied to what I produced for others. I began to remind myself that I had worth. You can do the same. You can start small. One quiet meal without a screen. One walk where you leave your phone behind. One page of thoughts written down without editing. These small acts add up, just like mine did.

Here in the quiet peace that I had built around myself, I learned to breathe again. Not the shallow, survival breaths I'd been living on, but the kind that fills your lungs and settles deep in your bones. I stopped running from my pain and began meeting it head-on. I read books I'd long meant to read, savoring familiar stories and making new memories as I did. Little by little, I began to find my courage. I started to hear my own thoughts without interference.

Fragments of Courage

One evening near the end of my stay, I found myself unsure what to paint. The sun was setting, and I carried my brushes, paints, and a small glass of water out to the porch. I set the glass beside my canvas and closed my eyes in meditation, letting the sounds of the mountains settle over me.

When I opened my eyes, I saw it, the glass casting fractured patterns of light across the blank canvas, scattering into delicate shapes and shifting colors. It stopped me cold. The beauty felt both fragile and infinite, here and gone in the same breath. I knew I could never recreate it perfectly, but I reached for my watercolors anyway, trying to hold on to what could not be held. Those moments of refracted, fractured light and color.

I wanted so desperately not only to capture that image of perfection, but also to grab for myself some part of that fleeting beauty. In that moment, it felt as if I had been holding my breath for so long that I had forgotten what it felt like to breathe deeply. To find love and acceptance for myself in my imperfect, fragmented state. The beauty of that moment, the shards of light interrupting each other; beautiful, fractured, imperfect -but somehow perfection.

In my journal that night, I wrote about finding fragments of courage in my day, calling it fractal courage.

This painting became "Fractal Courage," the foundation on which I began rebuilding my life. It taught me that courage doesn't usually arrive in one cinematic, life-altering moment. Real courage is fractured; made up of tiny, imperfect fragments. Small, almost invisible acts of bravery that, on their own, might seem insignificant. But when they're repeated, when they're layered, they form something unshakable. Fractal Courage became a bridge to return, one small, steady act at a time.

That's what this journey back to myself felt like: broken bravery. Shards of effort. Micro-acts of showing up, even on the days when showing up felt impossible. It wasn't about a single leap of faith. It was about hundreds of small steps, each one quietly daring me to believe in the possibility of more.

Every brushstroke, every honest word in my journal, every walk outside, every meal I chose to nourish my body with, every quiet moment I learned to embrace. Each was a microdose of courage. And together, they became the very thing I thought I'd lost forever.

A Door Cracks Open

I didn't know it at the time, but I was already doing the work of the next phase: recognizing my patterns, interrupting them, and slowly learning to create new ones. Fractal Courage was born here, in the daily decision to show up for myself in ways no one else could see. And over time, those small, hidden acts became the foundation for the life I'm living now.

Courage is not about proving anything to anyone; it's not loud or showy. It's about alignment. Choices that match the life I truly want for myself. I finally began to step into the driver's seat of my life. I can now decide where my path takes me. And it started here, with this experiment in stepping away from the noise.

When I look back at those 23 days, I can see the framework that held me together: *Rest, Retreat, Recharge.* They no longer felt like luxuries; they became the foundation of recovery. Each one was a quiet rebellion against the daily erosion of my life.

Rest became the foundation for lasting change. It was not just about sleeping in or taking time off. It was about giving myself permission to stop filling every moment with worry and self-criticism. It was learning to sit in stillness without guilt and to acknowledge when my body was tired. It was learning to teach my inner voice to respond with kindness instead of criticism. Rest reminded me that I did not have to earn peace. I could simply allow it.

Retreat invited me to hear my own thoughts again. It was not easy because silence revealed truths I had long drowned out with busyness, people-pleasing, and noise. In that quiet, I began to see how I had surrounded myself with people and patterns that were not safe or supportive. By stepping back, I began to reclaim my boundaries and edit my life. I learned that saying no was an act of self-respect and a way to begin again.

Recharge gave me permission to return renewed. This was where the quiet rebellion began to take shape. I started noticing small things again: the scent of rain, the weight of a book, a walk in fresh air. These moments were not grand gestures of self-care. They were simple choices that nourished me rather than drained me. With each one, I came closer to myself.

> *Together, Rest, Retreat, and Recharge became a continuous rhythm of recovery rather than separate steps. They reminded me that healing is not something we chase. It is something we practice, one breath and one honest choice at a time.*

These weren't sweeping changes; they were quiet steps, repeated until they began to feel like strength. They were simple, deliberate acts one after the other until they became a lifeline. They reminded me that recovery isn't one leap: it's a thousand tiny steps. Recovery, like bravery and courage, is fractal.

Looking back, just finding the strength to understand that I needed to change, to find a place to retreat, and to get out of bed each morning was more brave than I could see at the time. My hands trembled, and my mind screamed that I didn't have the strength for one more day, but courage was already there, quiet, unseen, steadying my breath. It was the kind that doesn't arrive with confidence or certainty; it shows up in shaking hands that still reach for the light.

If I could hold that version of myself now, I would thank her for teaching me what real courage feels like. **I would trace it like a scar, not to reopen the wound but to remember how it healed.** Every small act was a stone laid in the foundation of becoming. Each morning I rose was proof that survival itself is sacred.

Without realizing it, I was already noticing subtle yet powerful patterns. I caught myself reaching for chaos when I felt vulnerable, recognizing tiny triggers that pulled me away from my well-being. I didn't yet have a name for what I was doing, but I could feel it: these small decisions, stacked over time, would either lead me back to myself or leave me drifting in the dark. Recognizing my patterns wasn't about shame; it was about awareness. Each loop became a doorway back to myself.

A Quiet but Defiant Life

If you take anything from this chapter, let it be this: you do not need to disappear for 23 days to begin your own quiet rebellion of rebuilding and re-invention. You can carve out five minutes in your car before walking into work. You can take a walk without your phone. You can say "no" to one thing today. The point is not the size of the act. It's the choice to show up for yourself in ways you've been taught to ignore.

Healing isn't always about finding the "right" path; it's about creating space for yourself to try. For me, that space took the shape of a watercolor brush

Fractal Courage In Motion

Fractal Act: Embodied Courage

Choose one micro-act that affirms life: make your bed, drink water slowly, take a walk, write one honest line. When your hands tremble, place them over your heart and whisper, This is courage too.

At the end of the day, list three fragments of courage you noticed in yourself - they may be barely visible, but together they tell your story.

Fractal Practice: Fragments of Courage

Gather a small object that catches the light - a glass of water, a mirror shard, a stone, a piece of jewelry, anything that reflects or refracts light. Hold it in your hand and let the light move across your skin.

Take three slow breaths and notice what happens when light touches something imperfect.

In your journal, write or sketch where you feel fractured yet still beautiful. Ask yourself: What part of me is trying to hold the light today?

When you finish, leave the object where you can see it. Let it become your daily reminder that courage is not whole; it is gathered, piece by piece.

and a canvas that I washed clean every morning. The ritual was never about the art itself; it was about what the act taught me. That beauty can be temporary, mistakes can be part of the masterpiece, and letting go can be its own kind of creation.

Your outlet may not be painting. It could be coloring, sewing, photography, gardening, or anything that provides you with a way to make something that didn't exist before. The point isn't to make it last forever. The point is to return to it, again and again, until it becomes a pattern. A quiet rebuilding against the parts of you that once believed you weren't worth the time.

Creative expression is a bridge, connecting mind, body, and soul, pulling you into the present while also giving you permission to destroy, erase, or begin again. In its impermanence lies the lesson: you can change. You can start over. You can make something beautiful and then let it go. It's about finding perfection within the imperfect.

When you strip it down, that's what these 23 days were about: relearning how to live through small, repeated acts. Rest. Retreat. Recharge. Whether that act was a brushstroke, a deep breath, or saying no to something that drained me, I was creating a new pattern.

I didn't know it yet, but these simple repetitions - the showing up, the letting go - were laying the groundwork for the next stage of my journey. A stage where I would start to see the hidden patterns in my life… and begin the work of changing them.

Without yet understanding it, I was doing something powerful beneath the surface: I was starting to notice the subtle loops and reflexes that kept me stuck. Without naming them, I felt the pull of old patterns and, one decision at a time, began learning to choose differently.

In the next chapter, I'll take you deeper into this; into how I began to see the shapes of those patterns, how I learned to interrupt them, and how I started crafting new ones. But for now, know this: every small, brave choice you make is a seed. And when you plant enough of them, they grow into a life you can stand in without apology.

I found the courage, the audacity, to show up for myself in the middle of the storm, and you can too. I began the slow, deliberate work of coming back to life. This time, I decide what that life looks like, how it feels, and who I choose to share it with. And so do you.

Fractal Courage In Motion

Fractal Act: The Quiet Declaration

Turn self-recognition into an act of rebellion against invisibility. Find a mirror, a window, or even your reflection in a dark screen. Look at yourself — not to fix or assess — but to recognize who showed up today.

Place your hand gently over your heart and say, aloud or softly: "I am here. I am still becoming."

Let the words echo for a moment. They are not an affirmation; they are evidence.

Fractal Practice: The Defiant Kindness

Transform old narratives of "too much" or "not enough" into gentleness and pride.

Write one paragraph or create one image that celebrates something you used to criticize in yourself. Maybe it's your sensitivity, your hesitation, your persistence. Reframe it as a form of wisdom or resilience.

Title your page "Defiant Kindness."

Read it back slowly, as if you're speaking to the version of you who once believed you weren't enough.

Fractals Of Change

"You must let go to Become."
– R. King

When the Patterns Come Into Focus

I left the quiet reverie of my 23 days with more than rest and solitude. I left with clarity. The silence stripped me bare, showing me the patterns that had quietly shaped my life for years. It was in the stillness that I began to see how my choices, habits, and even the people I surrounded myself with had created a rhythm I didn't realize I was following. These weren't just random moments; they were repeating patterns, woven into the fabric of my life.

At the time, I didn't have words for it. I only knew that if I kept living the way I had been, I would keep losing myself. Looking back now, I understand that what I was stumbling into was a practice: the art of recognizing, interrupting, and creating patterns. These became the building blocks of my healing.

This chapter invites you into that practice, not as theory, but as a framework born of lived experience. I'll show you how I began to notice the hidden loops running my life, how I learned to stop them in their tracks, and how I started to replace them with rhythms that built me up instead of breaking me down. And the best part? You don't need to escape your life to start. You can begin exactly where you are, even in the middle of your chaos.

Once the noise stopped, I began to hear the truth beneath it and to see my life more clearly than ever before. My thoughts, my emotions, even my body had a language. I just hadn't been listening. I removed everything I could that distracted me, and in that rare quiet, I heard my soul, perhaps for the first time in my life.

The first step was learning to see. To notice the loops, I was running on repeat. I began to recognize the moments I reached for noise instead of silence, the ways I overcommitted instead of resting, and the habits that kept me small. Awareness was the beginning.

I had centered my daily life pre-sabbatical around what little I could control. When things didn't go to plan, I would spiral, lash out in anger, or withdraw. I began to see this pattern so clearly when I stepped away from my chaotic life. I started learning to let go, to relax my grip. I had to learn to let the results speak for themselves and stop the negative self-talk.

Learning to See Clearly

Pattern recognition is brutal. You see all the ways you've betrayed yourself. But it's also empowering. Because once you see it, you can interrupt it. The truth is, most of our patterns don't begin with us. They're handed down from childhood. The way our parents modeled love, safety, or survival. They are the stories we absorbed before we had the words to question them. Lived experiences that etched grooves into our nervous system, teaching us how to cope. Even if those coping mechanisms later became cages.

For most of us, the patterns we uncover were born from damaged people. Their wounds became lessons; their survival strategies became your training. And without realizing it, you carry those imprints into adulthood. Sometimes turning the hurt inward, other times passing it along to those you love most.

The devastation comes when you realize that even though you swore you'd do everything differently, the pattern persists. You tell yourself your circumstances are different, your choices are better, your intentions are pure. But then you catch yourself reacting in a familiar way, repeating what was done to you, and it feels like the floor drops out.

The most brutal truth to face was that my silence and self-erasure caused harm. By trying to keep the peace, I passed on pain. This was my reckoning, the moment I saw how survival can become complicity. I had become the damaged daughter raising damaged children.

Some patterns look like people-pleasing because you grew up in a home where love was conditional. Some look like silence, because speaking your truth once got you hurt. Others look like perfectionism, because you learned early that mistakes came at too high a cost. None of this started as betrayal; it began as survival. But as adults, survival isn't enough.

Seeing the pattern means reclaiming the power to choose. And once you see it, you can interrupt it - with action, with silence, with creativity. That interruption becomes the opening for something new: the daily practice of creating a different pattern, one that honors who you are becoming instead of who you were forced to be.

When you take a closer look at your own patterns, it's like standing under harsh light; you notice every scar, but also where healing has begun. Recognition hurts because it reveals both the damage and the doorway to change. That's why recognition can feel like betrayal and freedom at the same time. It breaks you open, but it also gives you the chance to stop the cycle. Because once you see them, your behaviors and reactions, you can choose to interrupt them. And from that interruption, you can begin to create something new.

This is where recognition begins. Before we can create new patterns, we have to catch ourselves in the old ones. For me, that meant noticing how quickly I reached for my phone when I felt uneasy, how easily I buried myself in busyness rather than grief, how I shaped my life to meet the needs of everyone but myself. I had hurt the ones I loved by retreating to my bed. Each of us will uncover a different list, yet the practice remains constant: recognize it, call it what it is, and pause before deciding whether it deserves your energy again.

At first, I didn't recognize the patterns. I thought I was a mess. But then I noticed the rhythm - the way I spiraled after a particular thought. The way shame always followed recognition. The way I disappeared after connection.

I began to see how much of my life had been shaped by others' expectations, by unspoken rules, by generational patterns. Early on, I learned that home was not safe. We performed in front of others to hide what happened at home. We built a pretend life at work, school, and church. Once we got behind closed doors, neglect, misdirection, gaslighting, and abuse were my

Fractal Courage In Motion

Fractal Act: The Living Canvas

Turn self-recognition into movement and creation. You have spent time looking inward — now let what you've discovered take shape outside of you.

Find a blank page, a canvas, or even a sheet of scrap paper. Choose a color, word, or image that feels true to this moment. Let your hand move without planning or perfection. You are not making art to display; you are letting your truth breathe.

When you're done, pause and study what you've made. Notice the lines, the tension, the light that slipped in anyway. Then close your eyes, take one slow breath, and imagine that same energy weaving through your life. This is how healing continues — not in silence, but in motion.

Fractal Practice: Map the Loops

The act of mapping transforms fear into awareness and awareness into agency - the heart of fractal healing.

In your journal, draw a simple circle. Inside it, write one pattern that you now recognize: maybe a way you retreat, overwork, control, or self-erase. Around the circle, write or sketch the moments that trigger this pattern. Don't analyze, just name them. On the outer edges, write possible interruptions: a breath, a boundary, a new choice.

Title your page "My Loops Are My Lessons."

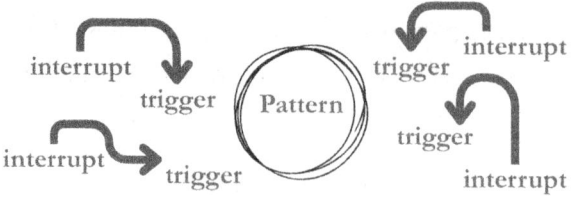

Each time you notice the pattern arise in daily life, imagine tracing that circle again; but this time, pause before completing it.

reality. This is where my 'pretend' life began.

I started asking: What do I want? What do I believe? What do I need? Why do I respond that way?

Fractal Courage isn't about becoming someone new. It's about remembering who you were before the world taught you to shrink, to stay small - Then choosing, every single day, to do one brave thing that reclaims that truth.

It begins with recognition: standing still in the life we've built, with the people we've chosen, and looking honestly at where we are. Taking stock of what we do, how we react, and the patterns that run on autopilot. From there, the work is to gently rewire those reactions into something better, a higher, truer version of ourselves.

Sometimes that means drawing boundaries. Sometimes it means removing people from our lives who bring harm, discomfort, or abuse. Recognition itself becomes the first courageous step. And if we let it, that step is enough to spark a catalyst for lasting change.

A Day that Changed Everything

Have you ever experienced a week that felt like a month, or lived a single day that felt like a year? For me, that day was May 10th, 2023. On that day, I realized two things with piercing clarity:

- I was sick - very, very sick.
- To survive, I had to let go of my then-husband.

Part of me grieved that truth, but another part of me rejoiced. I felt the faintest spark of a new life beginning. And yet, in that moment, I was untethered. Floating as if in outer space, unable to find gravity for the second time in my life. It was like waking from a coma into a world where everyone spoke a different language.

The decision to leave an abuser is rarely clean or simple. It can feel like choosing between two impossible options. Sometimes it feels like you must save yourself because you cannot save them. That day, I understood in my bones that there was no saving "us," no saving him without destroying myself. And for the first time, I chose me. That was the moment the fracture became a doorway. A choice that didn't look like triumph, but like truth. It was the smallest act of survival, and the beginning of becoming.

But it didn't feel like liberation. It felt like tearing, an unraveling, like pushing someone out of a lifeboat in the middle of the ocean. This was the person I had once believed I would die for. I wanted to believe he loved me in the same way, but that was part of that false reality; our public life was far different than our private life. Still, I had to save my life, even if it meant letting go of his.

All I knew was that survival required a choice, and I chose myself.

I began to recognize that while he said all the right things. It was the theatre of words, grand, sweeping, captivating. I was mesmerized by the stories he spun, the vivid pictures he painted, so full of promise. They became a constant misdirection, a kind of magic trick where I was always looking at the show instead of the truth. I lived in Neverland when I believed him, suspended in a world of words over actions. That's where I built my life: in a script that wasn't real.

It wasn't until much later that I realized the cruelty hidden in the beauty of those illusions. His words weren't love; they were camouflage. They kept me wandering through a false world, one that looked alive on the surface but was hollow underneath.

I often thought of the words attributed to Alice in Wonderland: *"You are a terribly real thing in a terribly false world, and that, I believe, is why you are in so much pain."* That line pierced me. Because that's exactly what it felt like, my truth crashing against a reality I had been convinced to believe in. The pain came not from my failure to love, but from living inside a performance that never matched what was behind the curtain.

The most devastating recognition that day was not simply that I had married a man who mirrored the very wounds of my childhood, but that I had allowed it to continue. I had chosen his words over my own truth and that of our children, again and again. I had accepted pain as love because my earliest programming taught me that love could look like harm. And that day, with the weight of my life pressing down on me, I saw clearly that his actions and inactions were not just failing to heal me; they were breaking me further.

What hurt the most was not him as he was, but the realization that I had betrayed myself. That I had abandoned my own needs in the name of saving him, in the name of keeping the story alive, in the name of loyalty to something that was never loyal to me. That was the fracture point - the moment of pattern recognition.

That day became more than just a decision; it was a pattern revealed. I could suddenly see the cycles I had been trapped in, the ways I kept repeating what I swore I'd never live through again. Recognition was brutal, but it was also a doorway to a new reality that I got to create. Because once you can see a pattern, you begin to loosen its hold, and you can begin to interrupt it. And once you interrupt it, you can create something new.

> **Fractal Reflection:**
>
> *If you could step outside of yourself and watch your life like a movie, which scenes would you want to replay, and which ones would you want to rewrite?*
>
> *What patterns would stand out to you most clearly?*

Experience is shaped by the meaning you give it. Every pattern you repeat, every habit you default to, comes from a story you once believed about who you are and what you deserve. The goal here is simple but not easy: to begin noticing the patterns that no longer serve you —the ones that quietly erode your peace or harm the people around you. Most of what we do each day runs on autopilot, guided by old conditioning. To change it, we first have to see it clearly. You cannot manage what you do not measure, and you cannot transform what you refuse to name. Our goal here is to identify patterns we repeat that impact our daily lives negatively.

Remember: Every reader's list will be different, but the practice is the same; see it, name it, pause before you feed it again.

Breaking the Script

Pattern recognition. **Pattern interruption.** Pattern creation.

That's what I started doing: interrupting. When I wanted to crawl back into bed, I stood up instead. When I wanted to numb out, I walked outside. Not for hours, just for a minute. Just long enough to create a fracture in the loop.

Those fractures became space. Space to choose. Space to breathe.

My first act of pattern interruption came when I cut the feed of noise I'd been using to numb, distract, and survive. We can't recognize the patterns that are hurting us until we strip away the static and give our minds room to notice them. Quiet is uncomfortable at first, but it's where truth gets loud.

Eventually, those interruptions became patterns of their own. I called them my anchors: journaling, eating breakfast in the morning sun, a slow walk around the block, and watercolors at night.

Each act wasn't loud. Each act wasn't enough on its own to call a transformation. But stacked together, day after day, they created something new. I was creating a path back to myself.

Fractal Courage isn't about burning it all down. It's about giving yourself permission to evolve. To start small and stay steady. I realized I was excavating, digging down through the rubble of my old life. What surfaced was the truth. Bravery isn't loud. Bravery is consistent. It's the act of facing yourself and learning to love and accept where you are, while looking forward to where you wish to go.

Letting Go to Become

As kids, we raced across the monkey bars, competing to see who could skip the most rungs. I worked up to skipping two, but I always feared missing the rung and taking the walk of shame to the back of the line. I learned early that if I focused on fear, I would fall every time. But when I focused on my goal instead of the fear, I could fly across the bars. My hands blistered, but I kept going.

I came to understand that the lesson was hidden in the swing itself: to move forward, you have to let go of the bar behind you before your hand connects with the next. For a split second, you're suspended, weightless, uncertain, hanging between what you've released and what you haven't yet reached. That breathless second, that's where courage is born, not in the safety of what you hold, but in the risk of reaching into the unknown.

Courage is built the same way, on pattern interruption. Refusing to repeat the reaction you've always had and replacing it with the tiniest act of rebellion.

The truth is, success, whether in business, healing, or recovery, doesn't belong to the smartest, the most charismatic, or the most beautiful. Success belongs to those who stay consistent. Consistency breeds change.

And when you're recovering from trauma, consistency feels impossible. It's like walking around with an entire nation of earthquakes inside while the rest of the world insists you look fine. So you mimic "fine," even though inside you are crumbling. Pattern interruption is how you stop pretending. It's how you begin again.

For me, the practice of breaking my days into quarters, simple routines repeated day by day, was my saving grace. What once felt impossible, like the weight of the world, became routine, even easy. Slowly, a day arrived when I didn't have to think about what to do next. I just got up and took that step.

Sometimes interruption is as simple as breaking the loop with surprise. I remember watching my oldest son spiral into panic, hands shaking, words racing faster than I could catch. He is on the spectrum, and these moments often felt like quicksand, pulling him deeper with every thought. One day, instead of trying to reason with him, I tried interruption. Out of nowhere, in the middle of his spiral, I said, "Do you know the Muffin Man?"

He froze. Then, without hesitation, he finished the next line from the movie Shrek. Then laughed, panic forgotten. Just like that, the loop broke. His mind unclenched, his body softened, and the storm passed.

That's the essence of pattern interruption: creating enough of a fracture in the spiral to make space for something else, humor, presence, possibility. It reminds me of that line from Alice in Wonderland, where the Queen tells Alice: *"Sometimes I've believed as many as six impossible things before breakfast."* What seems impossible, stopping a panic spiral, breaking an old destructive habit, suddenly becomes possible when you interrupt the expected script.

Art worked the same way for me. When I felt the pull toward old patterns, hiding in bed, numbing out, disappearing, I picked up a brush. It didn't matter what I painted. The act itself was an interruption. Color broke through the gray. The movement of the brush cut through the paralysis. And each time I washed the canvas clean, I reminded myself that nothing had to stay fixed, not even my pain.

That's the gift of interruption. It doesn't have to be dramatic. It might be a silly movie line, a splash of watercolor, a song on repeat, or simply stepping outside for a single deep breath. What matters is creating enough space to choose something different.

Micro Acts, Macro Courage

Creation is one of the oldest powers we carry as human beings. It's not just about art, music, or writing; it's about the daily choice to shape the world around us with intention. As Rick Rubin reminds us in The Creative Act: A Way of Being, creation is less about producing something and more about the way we choose to exist in each moment. To create is to resist stagnation. To create is to live intentionally, one moment at a time.

I often think of the Tibetan monks who spend days, sometimes weeks, creating intricate sand mandalas; breathtaking works of art made from nothing more than colored grains of sand. And then, once the mandala is complete, they sweep it away. It isn't destruction; it's devotion. A reminder that impermanence itself can be beautiful. That nothing is wasted when it teaches us how to begin again.

That same truth runs through our daily lives. Pattern creation isn't about sweeping, overnight transformations. It's not about chasing perfection or permanence. It's about small creative acts that become microdoses of

Fractal Courage In Motion

Fractal Act: Create the Fracture

Interruption through micro-action, courage as a lived moment. Choose one moment today to interrupt an old loop. When you feel yourself slipping into a familiar pattern - overthinking, scrolling, criticizing yourself - pause.

Do something unexpected:
- *Sing a single line from a song you loved as a child.*
- *Step outside and name three colors you see.*
- *Doodle a spiral on a napkin.*
- *Whisper, "I'm here."*

That interruption, however small, is your first act of rebellion. You're not trying to erase the pattern; you're creating space between stimulus and response - the birthplace of freedom.

Fractal Practice: Rewriting the Script

Turn reflection into practice. At the end of your day, write down one pattern you noticed.

Next to it, write what you did - or could do - to interrupt it. Then, complete this line:
"Tomorrow, when this pattern shows up again, I will choose to…"

Fold the paper. Keep it where you can see it - your desk, mirror, dashboard.
Let it remind you: **patterns lose power when they are named.**

courage. These acts, making a meal with care, sketching in the margins, choosing silence over reaction, journaling your pain instead of drowning it, or even closing one door and walking through another, create a rhythm. Over time, they build the scaffolding of a new life.

Pattern recognition shows us where we've been trapped. Pattern interruption breaks the cycle. But it's pattern creation; the daily choosing of new acts that gives us a future. Like the monks, we may sweep away what we've built one day, but the act of creating again becomes the courage that carries us forward.

Sometimes creation doesn't look like building something new; it looks like closing something old. Think of the doors you pass through every day, bedroom to kitchen, office to hallway, car to store. You walk through them without a thought, until one day, one of those doors becomes the last. The last time you cross a threshold that once defined you, the last time you carry a role, a relationship, or a routine that no longer serves you.

In that moment, a simple, ordinary act, turning a handle, stepping across, becomes extraordinary. You don't always recognize it while you're doing it. But later, looking back, you realize that closing that door was an act of courage. It was impermanent, like the sand mandalas - meant to dissolve, not to last forever.

That's the paradox: what feels like an ending is really the quiet birth of something new. Each closed door becomes a doorway into a life you're still creating. And the *courage lies not in knowing exactly what's ahead, but in choosing to step through anyway.*

For my journey, I chose to do what once felt impossible: leave my marriage and step into a future I couldn't yet see. When I finally made the decision, I realized something vital: the only power I had in that moment was the power to leave. I was still broken, still barely functioning, even with the rest and recharge of my sabbatical. I had no energy to build a plan, no capacity to map out the next chapter of my life. So I asked my sister if I could stay with her for six weeks. I needed a respite from the simple act of leaving, time to build that next step.

Your path will look different than mine. Most of you will not need to dismantle your entire life or leave a marriage to begin again. But all of us will face moments when the weight of staying is heavier than the risk of moving. That is the choice point, the door, the rung on the monkey bars, the boat pulled just close enough for you to climb into.

> *Fractal Courage isn't about dramatic leaps. It's about micro-acts of bravery, repeated daily, that accumulate into something unshakable. What matters isn't the scale of the step - it's that you take it, again and again. Healing doesn't demand perfection. It demands presence. And presence will always carry you farther than fear.*

Healing doesn't arrive. It accumulates, and sometimes scars will remain. They are reminders that we survived and we are still becoming.

I need to pause here and acknowledge something important: not everyone will be able to change their circumstances. Some of you may still be in homes, marriages, jobs, or family systems that feel suffocating. You may not have the option, or the safety, to walk away.

But here's the truth: even when you cannot change the larger circumstance, you can still create change in the micro. You can still plant seeds of fractal courage in the quiet corners of your day. You can choose to change how you respond, how you speak to yourself, how you carve out a single breath of silence in the middle of chaos. Those micro-acts matter. They build a scaffold of strength until, when the time is right, you can take the bigger steps.

Fractal Courage is not about escaping your life. It's about reclaiming pieces of yourself within it, one small act at a time.

Fractal Reflection:

Micro Act:

What is one small, repeatable act you could add into your day that nourishes you, even if it feels insignificant?

Macro Courage:

Where in your life are you clinging to a bar behind you—out of fear, habit, or obligation?
What might happen if you loosened your grip?

Reentry + Resurrection

"The real voyage of discovery consists not in seeking new landscapes, but in having new eyes."
– Marcel Proust

New Eyes, Same Life

Coming out of the sabbatical was far more complicated than going in. The quiet had changed me. Chaos now felt unbearable. For the first time in years, I could hear myself think and trust what I heard. I could feel my intuition again, and I began to recognize what "no" felt like in my body, and finally, I listened. Reentry was not seamless. Returning to daily life was not about stepping back into who I was before; it was about carrying this new awareness into a world that had not changed with me. The house, the job, the people all looked the same, but I was not the same. Only I had changed. Radically!

I did not want to go back to the life I had before. I could not. That version of me had died in the quiet. What returned was someone new, untested, but real. I carried new rituals, new rhythms, and most importantly, new boundaries.

When I stepped back into my old life, I realized that I was carrying new eyes. I could see the cracks I had once ignored, the patterns I had once excused, and the way I had betrayed myself to keep everyone else comfortable. That clarity was painful, but it also gave me the power to choose differently this time.

The sabbatical had stripped me down and rebuilt me piece by piece, but coming home was like walking back into a storm wearing new skin. I could see with clarity what no longer fit, but the world had not caught up to my transformation. I was untested, yet it felt like sitting for my PhD finals in life, right out of the gate.

This was no gentle transition. It was the real exam: could I hold on to fractal bravery, not just in the quiet of retreat, but in the noise of reality? Courage in retreat had meant stillness, surrender, and repair. Courage in reentry now meant boundaries, truth-telling, and holding steady when the world pushed back. The form had changed, but the rhythm was the same - small, repeated acts of bravery that carried me forward one deliberate breath at a time.

> *Fractal Reflection:*
>
> Pause today when you feel uncertainty. Take one breath and notice what part of you resists reentry.

Find Out What You Are Facing

You are not broken until you're ready. You are still breaking if you are not willing to face yourself and begin the work of change. Breaking is the daily destruction we allow when we remain in patterns that harm us. Only when that breaking is finished, when you are no longer willing to subject yourself to the same cycles, are you truly broken. And it is in that moment that you are finally ready to face yourself, to face the unknown, and to take the first step on the path toward becoming.

As the character Westley said to Buttercup in The Princess Bride, *"Life is pain, Highness. Anyone who says differently is selling something."* The truth is this: life always brings pain. The question is which pain are you willing to live with? The pain of staying small or the pain of growth? For me, I was already in pain. The pain of stagnation. The pain of inaction and apathy. The pain of being trapped in victimhood.

When the pain of staying the same outweighed the pain of change, I had to choose. My first inclination was to take drastic action, which led me to the bathroom that day. When I chose life, I knew I would be forced to walk into the unknown. Do I keep living inside the pain of my past, or do I step into the pain that comes with building a future? That choice was my crossroad. It was like fear itself. The same fear that had held me back could become a tool, a kind of fuel, to propel me into the uncharted.

It was my monkey bar moment. To move forward, I had to let go of the rung behind me before I could grasp the one ahead. For a moment, I hung in suspension, but it was there, in that space between letting go and reaching forward, that courage was born.

Reentry Isn't Seamless

The day I left the sabbatical, I had a dentist appointment, and I was leaving my husband. I had written a letter to remind him of his promise that if I ever needed to go, he would let me leave. That letter took me ages to write; even as I wrote it, I kept waffling on whether this was the right choice. That morning, I went to the dentist for an appointment I had booked nearly two months before, to deal with a cavity and a sensitive tooth. With a numb mouth, I drove to our apartment, packed the essentials I could fit into my car while he was still at work, and waited.

When he walked through the door, his face was eager to see me. In his mind, I was returning to him. I was shaking like a leaf. How do you leave someone who has been physically aggressive, manipulative, and controlling, and remain intact? I did not know which version of him I would meet. Would it be the quiet rage that smoldered until it exploded, or the gaslighting charm that tried to rewrite reality? I held the letter in my trembling hands and, as calmly as I could, asked for a divorce.

He didn't see it coming - though the signs had been there for months. I had begged, bargained, and explained. Leaving wasn't sudden; it was the slowest breaking of all. As I drove away, shocked that I had left unscathed (physically at least) my mouth still numb from the dentist, my phone began buzzing with his calls and texts. For a moment, I nearly turned the car around. His words, his shock, his sadness, almost pulled me back into that 'theater of words' that had trapped me for years. But I gripped the steering wheel with everything I had. At the first stop, I blocked his number and kept driving.

I drove for eight hours to my sister's home. The entire way, I sobbed, I screamed, I trembled, but I kept moving forward.

Looking back, I know I did two things right. First, I left the state so I would not be tempted to return in a moment of weakness. He also could not easily come after me. Second, I blocked his phone. He could still reach our children, but I refused to be drawn into calls or texts that would reopen old wounds. From that point forward, all communication about the divorce happened through email. I no longer entertained arguments or circular fights. There was nothing left to debate. I was done. My boundaries, though new and shaking, had passed that first test and finally became walls of stone.

> *Fractal Reflection:*
>
> *What is one boundary, one small act, or one safe step you can take today to protect your own healing? Write it down, and honor it as a promise to yourself.*

Restoration Not Regeneration

The intersection of healing and healed does not look like regeneration. For a long time, I confused the two. I thought healing meant getting back to the person I once was, the me before the car crash, before the marriage, before the wounds of childhood. I believed that if I worked hard enough, prayed hard enough, endured long enough, I could return to that version of myself. I thought healing was renewal, a way to reclaim what had been lost.

But healing is not that. Healing is not regeneration. Healing does not hand us back the life or the self we had before. Healing reshapes us - it requires dismantling before rebuilding. It is active, not passive; creative, not corrective. It calls us to unravel, to examine, to rebuild piece by piece. We must process loss and learn to let go. Healing asks us to face the wreckage honestly, to sit with the pain, and to let it carve away what can no longer remain.

That journey through pain changes us. It changes the way we see ourselves, the way we see others, and the way we move through the world. On the other side of healing, we do not return to who we were before. We come back differently, altered, marked by the cost, but stronger for it.

In other words, healing is a journey, not a return to who we were. We will never again be the person we were before the trauma, the injury, or the loss. That person has already been changed. On the path to healing, we come to know the cost, the sorrow, and the impact of what happened. On the other side of healing, we will always bear the scar. We will always carry the memory of what it cost to arrive here.

We live in an illusion when we wait for regeneration, for a restoration to the person we once were. I was caught in that spiral myself, angry and grieving what I thought I had lost forever. I tortured myself with the thought that I would never return to who I was before.

> ### Fractal Reflection: What Remains, What Restores
>
> *Where are you waiting for regeneration, for things to return to the way they were, instead of allowing for restoration?*
>
> *What scars, emotional or physical, still carry the memory of cost for you? Can you see them as proof of strength rather than reminders of loss?*

The truth is this: we are not meant to regenerate what was. We are meant to rebuild, restore what remains. To reclaim, reinvent, and renew.

The cost to restore is not small. We must process our terror, grief, anger, and fear. These are not signs of weakness, but symptoms of the damage that must be examined and tended to. They are part of the work of healing and restoration. To be restored to ourselves, we must accept that we will never be the same. We must also accept that the world around us, our friends, family, and colleagues, will only see the end result. They will see you as healed, the finished product of your journey, while never knowing the depth of what it cost you to get there. That alone can feel isolating. You may feel false, even fraudulent, because you know the price you paid, and they do not.

It is easy to get stuck in that awareness of cost, to circle back to the pain, and in doing so to forget how far you have come. But when you step outside of the wound, you begin to see something else: your strength, your resilience.

The sheer power it took to bring yourself here, you did that! You can do that again. And in the moments when it feels as though no one else understands, remember that you do. That knowledge is not a burden but a key. Imagine what more you can do with that power now unleashed, carrying you forward into the future, ready for whatever trial comes next.

In my design career, I worked on the expansion and restoration of a State Capitol building. The project spanned several years. Our team was tasked with restoring the building to its intended beauty, undoing decades of neglect and careless expansion. We scraped through layers of paint to uncover the original colors, sourced tile manufacturers to repair broken floors, and traced marble panels back to quarries overseas to match new stone to old.

The final product was a restoration. It was not perfect. The architects & designers could point to every break in pattern, every door that had been replaced, every detail we could not recreate exactly. Yet the building stood beautiful and whole, not because it was returned to its untouched state, but because it was renewed.

We must do the same with ourselves. Healing is restoration, not regeneration. We must be willing to let go of what cannot be recovered, to honor what must be changed, and to see beauty in the scars that remain. Our finished selves are not flawless, but they are strong, resilient, and real. The work of healing is to stop chasing the impossible return to what was, and instead embrace the imperfect, restored beauty of what we are becoming.

Finding your Fractals

For me, resurrection wasn't loud. It wasn't a triumphant moment of rebirth. It wasn't one grand sweeping act of courage. It looked like brushing my hair, making my bed, eating a meal, and sitting at the table instead of hiding under the covers. These weren't glamorous acts. But they were steady ones. And steady is what brought me back to life.

Journaling and painting became my bridge back to myself. They were both outlet and balm for a soul still learning how to breathe again. The work I began in those twenty-three days started a transformation that is still unfolding. Healing did not end when the sabbatical did. I am still somewhere

Fractal Courage In Motion

Fractal Act: Honor the Scar

Transform recognition of pain into reverence for endurance. Choose one part of your story, body, or memory that still feels marked by what you've endured. Sit with it - place a hand over that space if it feels right - and name what it gave you. Strength. Compassion. Wisdom. A sharper instinct for truth.

Whisper or write: "I honor what remains."

The act is not about erasing the damage. It's about reclaiming the scar as proof of life, not evidence of failure.

Fractal Practice: Rewriting the Script

Move from passive reflection to creative rebuilding. In your journal, draw or describe something you've rebuilt: a relationship, a home, a sense of self. Note what could not be restored and what emerged in its place.

Then write this reflection:
"What if the cracks are the design?"

Each week, return to one area of your life where you've been waiting for regeneration: a past self, relationship, or dream - and instead ask, "How might I restore what remains?" Over time, this becomes your practice of restoration - not chasing the past, but building something truer from its foundation.

in the middle of it, still learning to let go of what was and to trust what is forming. The tools and insights I found in that quiet continue to shape me. They influence who I allow into my life, how I spend my time, and how I define success. These days, I find it in simple moments of peace, in mornings that begin with curiosity instead of fear, and in the quiet knowing that even without arriving, I am becoming.

That is the heart of **Fractal Courage**. It is not about waiting for one defining act of bravery. It is about continuing to do the small practices, day after day, until they take root. Healing means learning to spot the patterns that are sabotaging you; the ways you destroy yourself, and choosing to interrupt them.

At first, interruption feels unnatural, even impossible. But when you replace a destructive loop with a new act, something consistent and repeatable, you begin to build a different life: one choice, one action, one moment of showing up for yourself at a time. Over weeks and months, those choices add up. They become steady ground where chaos once lived.

Fractals are not glamorous; they are quiet revolutions. They are the smallest acts of bravery, repeated until they become your foundation. This is how you rewire your patterns and come back to life.

> *Fractal Reflection:*
>
> *What is one destructive pattern you can recognize in yourself today? How does it show up in your daily life?*
>
> *What is one small, repeatable act you can use to interrupt that pattern?*

Carrying the Quiet Back With You

For me, re-entry was about taking what I learned in silence and weaving it into the noise of everyday life. Bringing that stillness into my commute to work and the rigors of daily life. For you, once you start making these shifts, you will find that nothing around you may have changed, but you have. The task now is to hold onto that change when the storm closes in again.

My reentry led to dramatic immediate change. I left my husband of 23 years, I stopped working with toxic clients, and began to set boundaries and build bridges with my children. I continued to get out of bed and face each day with whatever energy I could muster. Each of these daily practices became a quiet vow to live differently and proof that I had the strength to make lasting change. Slowly, I began to see a new and exciting future for myself. A future that now opened wide to allow me to become that version of myself I had hidden for so long.

The silence I started during my sabbatical was not meant to stay locked in a cabin in the mountains. It had to come home with me. That meant learning how to create quiet in the middle of the noise, between emails, in the carpool line, even while folding laundry. I learned that the power of silence was not in its location, but in my willingness to choose it. Even when the world around me refused to slow down, I could still pause, take one breath, and remind myself: this is what it feels like to hear my own voice.

Every chapter of this journey builds on the last. The Collapse taught you that denial is not survival, and how to find truth in chaos. The Quiet Rebellion showed that silence and small choices are powerful acts of defiance. Fractals of Change revealed that courage grows through consistent, repeated acts, not in a single grand moment. Now, Reentry asks you to take all of these pieces and weave them into a life that will hold.

Your task is not to replicate my sabbatical. It is to create your own, inside the fabric of your everyday life. To find the cracks in your schedule where quiet can enter. To notice the destructive patterns that keep you spinning and interrupt them with one simple act. To choose creativity over consumption, rest over burnout, connection over isolation.

None of these choices will feel glamorous. They may not even be noticed by anyone else. But you will notice. And over time, the sum of those quiet, steady acts will become the new ground you walk on.

Fractal Courage In Motion

Fractal Act: Return to the Table

Transform daily practice into sacred routine. Choose one small, steady act that helps you meet yourself where you are today. It could be simple, making your bed, sitting at the table to eat, or lighting a candle before you journal. Let the act itself become a declaration: I am still here.

Repeat it daily, especially on the days that feel heavy or hollow. These are not gestures of perfection. They are quiet proofs of life - the kind that rebuild your sense of self one ordinary moment at a time.

Fractal Practice: Carry The Quiet

Finding the inner quiet of retreat within the noise. Find one place in your daily routine to invite stillness back in. It could be the pause before answering an email, the silence after turning off the car, or the breath you take before speaking. In that moment, ask yourself: What does peace sound like right now?

End your day by writing one line that begins with: "Today, I returned to myself when…" Over time, these lines become a quiet map back to your center — proof that healing is not finished, but in motion.

Stepping Into The Unknown

The truth is this: life will not pause to give you a perfect moment to start. The chaos, the obligations, and the unfinished business will still be there. Resurrection happens in the middle of it all. It happens in the promise you keep to yourself when no one else is watching. That is where your courage grows roots.

You have already seen that collapse is not the end. You have already proven that rebellion can begin quietly. You have already felt how small acts of bravery, repeated, begin to reshape your life. Now resurrection asks you to gather those lessons and live them out loud, not once, but every day. This is how you rise; not as the person you once were, but as the person you are becoming.

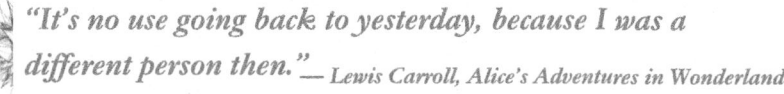

"It's no use going back to yesterday, because I was a different person then." — Lewis Carroll, Alice's Adventures in Wonderland

I once believed that healing meant returning to who I was before the breaking. But what I continue to learn is that true becoming happens through release. The same letting go that began in the quiet of retreat has become a daily act of faith. I no longer chase the life I lost. I build the life I choose.

I am not healed, but I am healing, and I have tools now. My promise is simple: I will never abandon myself again. Even when the world shifts around me, I will stay rooted in my own orbit. My work is no longer to strive for perfection, but to live as the woman I am still becoming, one steady, imperfect act of resurrection at a time.

In the end, resurrection is not a finish line. It is a rhythm. It is the steady return to yourself in the middle of the noise, the choice to rise even when no one sees it. The quiet courage to stay present, to keep showing up, to trust that every small act is part of a larger becoming. You are not defined by what was broken. You are defined by the strength it took to rise.

I was not healed. But I was healing, and I had tools now. The commitment I made was this: I will never abandon myself again. Even if the world shifts around me, I will remain rooted in myself. My orbit is

mine to protect, and I will welcome only those who honor it.

Fractal Reflection:

Who or what belongs inside your orbit, and what needs to be released from it?

The Goodbye Gap - The Framework Of Becoming

"The Goodbye Gap is the space between who you were and who you are becoming. It is not failure; it is the forge."
— R. King

The Space Between

Every transformation begins with a choice. But between the decision to change and the reality of living differently lies a fragile space I call the Goodbye Gap. It is the space where old habits tug at your sleeves, where the familiar feels warm and safe even as it begins to suffocate you. The air there is thick with hesitation, charged like the moment before a storm breaks. It's where the comfort of what you know whispers louder than the call of what could be. The Goodbye Gap is where courage is tested. Not in the moment you make that first brave choice, but in the moments that follow, you must decide again and again.

I wish I could say that healing in the middle of real life, the daily chaos and obligations, old patterns, family, and work was smooth. It wasn't. Healing is not linear. It is a process of progress and relapse, of courage one day and collapse the next. The difference was that now I had tools. When I stumbled, I recognized it for what it was - a spiral, not a failure. And instead of being consumed, I could stop, interrupt the pattern, and take a micro-step back toward center.

As part of my healing journey back to the new version of myself, I found that there lies a gap between where we are going and where we are coming from. The Goodbye Gap, so to speak. I don't think enough gurus talk about this, the distance from decision to transformation. It often feels like a pendulum; you get so far in recovery and healing, and then something pulls you back. A trigger, something that reminds you that you are not done healing.

For me, it happened when I least expected it. I thought I had defused the majority of my triggers. Those moments, scents, thoughts, or people who try to lure you back into complacency. Though I had begun to build a muscle around what I felt were my weaknesses. I found that there were days, weeks, or months when it felt like those weaknesses would spring back with a vengeance and overwhelm me.

I got angry at myself, thinking that there wasn't enough progress given the time I had left my marriage, or began to unravel my agoraphobia. I would let my inner voice speak again, that voice that told me I was worthless, that I had just wasted all this time and gotten nowhere.

This is the space where we have a choice: fall back into old patterns or keep moving. Give in to the temptation that says the cost of change is no longer worth the price. Or we can choose again, moment by moment, to keep on going. To pick back up. Pull out our tools and tricks and learn to start again. Every setback is not a failure. It is evidence of the journey, the wear and tear on our soles. The evidence of the friction of fighting back for the life we want to create - to become. The mileage is the proof that the journey is worth it, that it is working, that you are growing.

When you decide to let go of what no longer serves you, the change does not happen instantly. The world around you may look the same, yet you feel entirely different inside. This in-between place can feel unbearable, like living in two realities at once. The Goodbye Gap is where you begin to practice your new identity, even when everything around you tries to pull you back into the old one.

Breaking Old Agreements

I found that a key to understanding how to navigate and even accept the Goodbye Gap starts by making and keeping promises to myself. A promise to continue to strive for that final yard line where real change takes root and replaces old patterns.

Most of us fall into the destructive pattern of breaking promises to ourselves. We do it so often that our inner voice stops believing us. Without realizing it, we prove to ourselves over and over again that we are not worth the effort.

That pattern corrodes our spirit. The way back begins with establishing the opposite, not to the world, but to yourself.

Making and keeping even the smallest promises becomes a way of showing up for yourself. It may sound simple, but if you have lived in the spiral of neglecting your own needs, it can feel impossible. Yet every time you follow through, you send a message deep into your body and mind: I matter. My word has value! I can trust myself again.

This is not just self-care. It is reprogramming. Each kept promise rewires your hardwiring, builds your reserves, and strengthens your foundation. It creates space for you, not the version of you that only serves others, but the one who is capable of living fully and giving from abundance instead of depletion. When you learn to keep promises to yourself, you reclaim your worth.

> **Fractal Reflection:**
>
> *What is one small promise you can make to yourself today?*
>
> *List several ways to make sure you keep it.*

Relapse is Not Failure

The Goodbye Gap is messy. You will relapse. You will stumble. You may return to patterns you swore you were finished with. But relapse is not failure; it is feedback. It is a signpost showing you where your deepest wounds live and where your greatest healing is still needed. Every time you stop, notice, and choose again, you are building resilience.

Practicing Courage in the Gap

Courage in the Goodbye Gap does not look like a single sweeping act. It looks like micro acts of bravery. When the old voice says, 'You cannot,' you whisper back, 'Watch me!' Each act of defiance against the old pattern becomes a brick in the bridge that carries you across the Gap.

You must learn to rely on yourself for true, lasting progress to take shape. I had to learn that no one else could do this for me. For years, I had forgotten how to trust myself. Maybe it was the result of constantly breaking promises to myself, or the erosion of self-worth that taught me to rely on others to fix what I refused to face. But true healing demanded ownership. It meant recognizing that the same dependency that had once kept me safe had also kept me small. No one could climb this mountain for me. The climb was mine alone.

Getting to Shore

In my young adult life, I worked for a whitewater rafting company on the Salmon River. One afternoon during spring runoff, a trainee lost control of our raft, sending us straight into a bridge pylon under construction. The impact launched us all into the icy waters of that early spring snowmelt. I was pulled into an undertow until I felt my lungs would burst for want of air. Then I remembered something we were taught in training: Fetal, then spread eagle. When you are caught in an undertow, first curl in, gather your energy, calm your breath, and wait for your moment. Then, when the current shifts, extend outward with everything you have and swim hard for the surface.

As I did so, I surfaced gasping and stunned! My skin burning from the cold. When I saw the rescue boat approach, a rope arced perfectly through the air and landed beside me. For a brief moment, I felt saved.... until I realized no one had anchored the other end of the rope to the rescue boat. I was clinging to a lifeline that led to nowhere.

Panic set in. The current was strong, and my limbs were starting to fail me. The freezing water began to shut down my body. As this was the last training run of the day, many of us had removed our wetsuits, myself included. This left me without any protection against the effects of the frigid water; hypothermia would quickly set in. I made up my mind to get to shore; this would not be my end. Somehow, despite a body slow to respond to my command to swim, I made it to shore miles downriver. Trembling but alive. That rhythm of surrender and power saved my life.

That moment became my metaphor for healing. When the current of life drags you under, it is instinct to flail. But real strength begins with stillness, with contracting long enough to find clarity before expanding into motion again. Every time you feel yourself slipping backward, remember it is not weakness to pause. The pause is part of your power.

The Goodbye Gap is no different. The undertow of old habits will pull hard. You will lose your footing, question your strength, and reach for lifelines that no longer hold. But if you can pause, gather yourself, and then push forward, just one strong, deliberate movement. You will find your way back to shore. Movement, however small, is what saves you.

Each of us has the strength to rescue ourselves. Yes, support matters, friends, therapists, and family. However, the decision to rise must come from within. You survived what once tried to drown you. You are here, reading these words. That is proof of your strength. Let that truth carry you forward into lasting change.

> *Fractal Reflection:*
>
> *Where are you standing in your own Goodbye Gap right now?*
> *What part of your life feels suspended between who you were and who you are becoming?*
>
> *What lifelines are you still holding that no longer lead anywhere?*
>
> *What does crossing the gap mean for you?*
> *Imagine your version of the shore—what would it feel like to arrive, even if just for a moment?*

Crossing the Gap

The Goodbye Gap is not the end of your story. It is the beginning of your practice. The decision to change opens the door, but only action will carry you through it. This part of the journey is about holding steady, about building a pattern of small, repeated acts that remind you who you are becoming.

Crossing the Goodbye Gap does not mean you never look back. It means you keep walking forward, even when you stumble. It means learning to trust that the ground beneath you is being built by your own hands, one micro act, one promise, one breath at a time.

In those early days, I began to remember what it felt like to want to live again. When I left the bathroom that day, I was still shattered. The sabbatical became the ABCs for my life, the foundation I built from. Relearning how to breathe, how to eat, how to see, how to be. It was the practice of becoming whole again, not so I could save others, but so I could stand in my own life and love from a place that was healthy and true.

Healing taught me that courage isn't found in one sweeping act of change. It is built slowly, through consistency and self-compassion. What once felt impossible, to say no, to set a boundary, to leave what was destroying me, eventually became as natural as breathing.

That day I learned to save myself on the river taught me that same truth. Sometimes the lifeline you are waiting for will never come. Sometimes you are holding a rope to nowhere. In those moments, you must go inward first. Contract, gather yourself, breathe, then take the bold action to swim for the shore. Contract, then expand. Rest, then rise. That cadence is what crossing the gap looks like in real life.

You already know how to do hard things. You have survived every impossible moment that brought you here. Now, it's time to keep choosing yourself, again and again, until courage feels like your natural state.

The Becoming

There is no arrival point on this journey. There is only movement. One act of courage, then another. The bridge across the Goodbye Gap is built by your own hands, one stone, one promise, one choice at a time.

So take a deep breath. Look back only to see how far you have come. The rest of your life is waiting. Wide open, unformed, and yours to create.

The Goodbye Gap taught me that letting go is not the end of transformation, but its threshold. Standing there - between the life I was leaving and the one still forming -I began to see that healing wasn't about waiting for certainty,

Fractal Courage In Motion

Fractal Act:

Teach your nervous system what resilience feels like. When the current of the Goodbye Gap pulls you under - the overwhelm, the relapse, the fear - do what the river taught you:

Stop fighting for just a moment. Curl inward. Breathe deeply into your belly. Then, when your breath steadies, open your arms - literally stretch them wide - and imagine pushing toward the light.

Fractal Practice:

Create a simple two-column journal page:

Left side → Old Patterns That Pull Me Back.
Right side → New Acts That Move Me Forward.

Each time you notice yourself repeating an old loop, write it down and pair it with one tiny act of interruption. Over time, this list becomes your personal "Bridge Across the Gap" - a living map of your becoming.

but about learning how to live inside the unknown.

Each time you recognize a trigger or interrupt an old pattern, you are laying another stone across the Gap. Every moment you choose differently, you build your path forward, one conscious creative act at a time. That is how you reach across the space between who you were and who you are becoming. The Goodbye Gap was never just an ending; it was the work of building a new beginning in real time. Every stumble, every pause, every rise was practice. The truth is, every crossing prepares you for what comes next. You were already creating the framework long before you realized it, and now, it's time to live inside it.

The Framework of Becoming

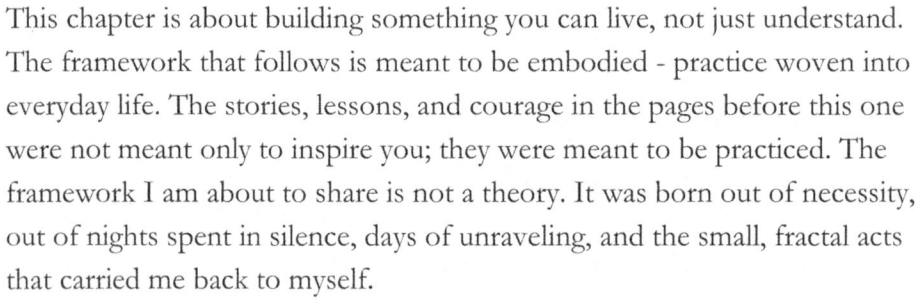

"You must do the things you think you cannot do."
— *Eleanor Roosevelt*

This chapter is about building something you can live, not just understand. The framework that follows is meant to be embodied - practice woven into everyday life. The stories, lessons, and courage in the pages before this one were not meant only to inspire you; they were meant to be practiced. The framework I am about to share is not a theory. It was born out of necessity, out of nights spent in silence, days of unraveling, and the small, fractal acts that carried me back to myself.

Your sabbatical may not look like mine. You may never be able to leave for 23 days. Most of us can't. But you can still create your own new beginning, right where you are, inside your current life.

Here we will review the principles of Rest, Retreat, and Recharge. This is your way back to yourself, and it begins with three pillars.

Rest: Restorative Stillness

Rest is more than sleep. It is permission to stop the endless striving, not the kind that helps you grow, but the kind that strips you bare and burns you out. Rest goes deep into the nervous system. It teaches your body that you are safe, that you do not have to run forever. True rest goes deeper than closing your eyes; it is the choice to soften into stillness, to allow your nervous system to reset, to show your body that it no longer has to live on high alert.

When you practice restorative stillness, you are teaching yourself safety. You are unlearning the constant demand to go, do, and achieve.

As the poet David Whyte reminds us, *"Rest is the conversation between what we love to do and how we love to be."* Rest is not a luxury. It is not wasted time. It is medicine for the soul.

Rest will look different for each of us. Letting your brain take a break from constant "what ifs" and "what's next." Even five minutes of not striving can feel like a release. Allowing yourself to imagine, wander, or be curious without needing an outcome. The point is not what it looks like, it is how it restores.

Fractal Reflection:

What does true rest look like for you, not the idealized version, but the kind that actually restores you?

How would your body respond if you gave it permission to pause without guilt?

Retreat: Choosing Quiet in the Chaos

Retreat does not always mean packing a bag or leaving your life behind. Retreat is not about geography; it is about intention. It is the deliberate act of choosing yourself amidst the noise.

Retreat is as simple as closing a door for five minutes. Find moments of quiet wherever you are. When you step away from the demands of others, you begin to hear the steady tempo of your own heartbeat again. These are small sanctuaries, but they matter. Create a pocket of stillness in the middle of the chaos and claim it as your own. It is in those moments of stillness before reaction where you begin to build that bridge toward that new you.

This is where the rebellion continues, not in dramatic acts. It is in the courage to pause, to step aside, to refuse to be consumed.

> *Fractal Reflection:*
>
> *Where in your daily life can you carve out a moment of retreat, even if it is only five minutes?*
>
> *What noise or distraction do you most often use to avoid silence, and what would it feel like to put it down?*

Recharge: Learning to Love Where You Are

Recharge happens when you look at your life with new eyes. It begins with gratitude for where you are now. It is about rediscovering what brings joy, purpose, and renewed energy. It means letting go of what no longer serves you and learning to love yourself in this moment, even if nothing has yet changed. Recharge happens when you create small, repeatable moments of renewal.

To recharge is to choose presence. It is the courage to see where you are right now and decide that this moment is enough to begin again. It does not require the perfect setting, the perfect timing, or even the perfect you. It only requires willingness.

Recharge is also about repetition. These rituals do not need to be complicated. They only need to be consistent. Recharge is not a luxury. If you practice it faithfully, it will begin to carry you when you feel you cannot carry yourself.

> *Fractal Reflection:*
>
> *What consistent, repeatable act of renewal could become your anchor?*

How can you create your own version of Rest, Retreat, and Recharge without leaving home?

Find Out What You're Facing

Finding out what you are facing means stripping away the illusions. It means naming the weight you carry, the wounds, the patterns, the burdens that you've normalized for too long. Abuse, neglect, grief, toxic relationships, endless obligations: all of it shapes how you move through the world. When you pretend it isn't there, it owns you. When you name it, you begin to reclaim yourself.

This work is not about judgment. It is not about calling yourself broken or weak. It is about honesty. It is about saying: This is what I am carrying. This is what has shaped me. This is what I no longer want to choose.

You may discover that some of what you carry is not even yours. Some are patterns inherited from family, wounds absorbed from people who were too damaged to love you well. You may find you are repeating behaviors you swore you would never repeat. That recognition can be devastating. But it is also where change begins. **You cannot rewrite a story until you are willing to read the one you are in.**

Discover What You Love

Give yourself permission to explore creative sparks, small joys, and practices that feed you. Healing often begins with noticing what stirs your soul. It may be art, music, writing, sewing, gardening, photography, or cooking. The medium does not matter. What counts is the act of creating. Creation itself is a form of healing, a quiet rebellion against the patterns that once silenced you.

Allow yourself to make something that will not last. Build and destroy, practice impermanence. Each time you create, you remind yourself that transformation is possible, that something new can rise from what once was broken.

For me, art was both interruption and resurrection. Painting became the way I stopped the spiral, the moment I could breathe again. For you, it might be coloring with your children, photographing the sky, planting seeds, or writing a page no one else will read. The point is not talent. The point is to choose creation over collapse, to use color, sound, or texture as a way to come back to yourself.

These small acts are not hobbies: they are lifelines. They remind you that you are more than what you have endured. They anchor you in the present and prove, again and again, that beauty can rise from brokenness - a declaration: I am still here, and I am still becoming.

Learn to Love Where You Are

Acceptance is not the end of the journey; it is the grounding from which all growth begins. It is the culmination of everything you have practiced: the rest, the retreat, the recharging, the pattern interruptions, and the courage to begin again. Loving where you are is the moment those practices take root. It is when healing becomes less about striving for a destination and more about inhabiting your life as it is.

Loving where you are is choosing to see your life through new eyes; it does not mean pretending everything is perfect. It means choosing to see your life without filters of shame, regret, or comparison. It is the quiet act of acceptance. It is the decision to stand in your present reality and say, "This is where I begin."

Acceptance is not resignation. It does not mean you stop reaching or desiring more. It means you build from truth rather than illusion. Acceptance says, "This is my ground, my skin, my life today." From that ground, you can grow. If you keep waiting until conditions are ideal, you will never begin.

When you stop resisting what is and start listening to what it can teach you, life begins to unfold differently. You stop waiting for perfect conditions to start. You recognize that transformation was never about the distance traveled but about the depth of presence.

To love where you are is to allow yourself to rest within your own becoming. You may not conquer the world every day, but each time you pause and breathe, you affirm: I am still here. I am still becoming.

Imperfectly Perfect

Healing does not happen in one sweeping act. Healing unfolds through repetition - tiny acts that slowly stitch courage back into your body. The Rest Retreat and Recharge framework is not a prescription; it is an invitation. It asks you to claim a few minutes of quiet, to give your body the kindness of stillness, to find one thing that nourishes your spirit and return to it again and again.

Your life may not allow for sabbaticals or mountain cabins. But it does allow for choices. And those choices add up. One breath. One pause. One act of creation. These are the fractals that become courage. You are choosing a way back to yourself. And the truth is, you already have what you need. Your courage is not somewhere out there; it is within you, waiting for you to take the next step.

Healing is not about waiting for the perfect time or place. It is about choosing, today, to begin again. Your version of a sabbatical may consist of small acts of pattern interruption every day. It does not need to look dramatic to be powerful.

This journey started when you bought this book. Now it's time to choose a way back to yourself. The framework I have given you here in these pages is a starting place. It is both an invitation and a challenge. To keep showing up. To keep interrupting the patterns that hold you hostage. To keep creating the micro acts of bravery that add up to courage, to change.

If you want more guidance, the **Fractal Courage Workbook: The Sabbatical for the Soul, A 90-Day Journey to Becoming** was created to walk alongside you day by day. It gives you prompts, exercises, and practices to help you live this framework in real time. But even without it, you have what you need. The path is not out there - it is inside you.

And when the days feel heavy, when the spiral pulls at you again, remember: You already know how to return. One step. One breath. One choice at a time.

Start where you are, with what you have. Stay steady. Stay present. Keep showing up. And when the world tells you to stay small, when the chaos tries to pull you back under, remember: you have already chosen differently once. You can do it again.

And when you do, remember this:

You have already lived through what was meant to break you, and yet you are still here. That alone is proof of your strength. You've learned what it means to hang between the bars of fear and becoming, to let go of the old rung before the next one appears. You've felt the pull of the river, the cold weight of despair, and still you kicked toward the surface. Survival was your first act of courage; now it is time to rise.

But rising does not mean you will never fall again. There will be days when the old patterns whisper, when the current tugs at your feet, and the rungs feel too far apart. That is not failure; it is the rhythm of becoming. You are not here to resurrect what was. You are here to restore what remains, to rebuild from truth, not illusion. Let go of what no longer serves you. Accept what was, and from that ground, begin again.

Each act of creation, whether it's a brushstroke, a line in your journal, or a simple breath of focus, is how you practice healing in real time. This is not about making something perfect or lasting. It is about showing up, creating, and letting go. Paint just to see the color move. Write just to hear your own thoughts. Build, then release. Art for its own sake teaches you to stop gripping so tightly and to allow what you create and what you feel to come and go. That is how restoration works.

You will build this life not all at once, but moment by moment. See your world as it is, not as you wish it had been. Then, from that truth, start again. Rise through the repetition. Create through the chaos. Love where you are, and let your small, steady acts become the architecture of your restoration.

Final Reflection

 Before you turn this page and step back into your life, take one slow breath.

You made it here.

You stayed.

You told the truth.

And that is the beginning of becoming.

To the Ones Crossing the Gap

If you have made it to this page, it means you stayed with me through the hard parts of this story. You witnessed my unraveling and my rebuilding, and I hope somewhere in these pages you found a piece of yourself. A reminder that you are not alone in this work.

If you are reading this and you feel caught between the life you have lived and the one you ache for, I want you to hear me clearly: I know that space. I have lived in that stretch of uncertainty, where everything feels too familiar and too foreign all at once. The gap is not a sign that you are failing. It is a sign that something inside you is shifting, reaching, loosening its grip on what was.

You are not meant to make this leap in one clean motion. Change rarely works that way. You move forward through the small, shaky moments. They can be as simple as the breath you choose to take instead of shutting down, the truth you whisper instead of swallowing, the promise you keep to yourself when no one else sees. If today feels heavy, let it be heavy. Rest is still movement. Pausing is still progress. I want you to know this: the person you are becoming is not lost. They are already inside you, waiting for space, waiting for honesty, waiting for you to stop abandoning yourself. You do not have to create a new version of you from scratch. You only have to return.

If you are standing in your own Goodbye Gap right now, unsure of what comes next, please hear this: you are not supposed to be farther along than you are. Healing is not a race. It is a return. And returns take time.

I know what it feels like when the old patterns tug at your sleeves, when you slip back into behaviors you swore you had outgrown. I have been there. I am still here, doing this work with you. The gap is messy. It is uncomfortable. And it is worth it.

When you stumble, because you will, acknowledge it honestly and gently. Then do the work you already know how to do. Find your monkey bar moment, where you let go of the rung behind you even before the next one appears. Find your river moment, when you curl inward, gather your strength, and then push toward the surface again. Create the smallest interruption in your spiral, just enough space to choose differently. Every setback is not a failure. It is a signpost. It shows you where one more fracture is waiting to be healed.

Some places inside you will mend quickly. Others may take years. That is not a flaw.

That is proof that you are crossing the gap, not by running or leaping, but by choosing yourself again and again.

As you go, remember this: peace does not arrive all at once. It comes in moments at first, a steady breath, a promise you keep to yourself, a truth spoken aloud, a boundary you own, a small act of creation that reminds you who you are. Over time, those moments grow into a life that feels open, honest, and entirely your own.

I hope you leave this book knowing that your future is not something you have to fear. There is peace ahead for you. There is clarity. There is strength you have not yet tapped, and joy you have not yet met. Most importantly, there is a version of you already waiting on the other side of this work.

You are worth the effort it takes to reach toward that version of yourself. And until you can believe it fully, *borrow my belief:*

You are not broken. You are becoming.

And you are not doing that alone.

Continue Your Journey

Stay Connected. Keep Becoming.

Continue Your Journey. Your healing does not end here. You now have the language, the practices, and the courage to begin again — but the path becomes easier with structure and support.

Go deeper with the **Fractal Courage Workbook: The Sabbatical for the Soul — A Journey to Becoming**

This 90-day guide expands the concepts in this book through:
✓ *Daily micro-practices*
✓ *Art-based healing*
✓ *Pattern recognition + interruption*
✓ *14-day milestone check-ins*
✓ *A rhythm of Rest, Retreat, Recharge, and Rise*

Looking for accountability and community?

Join the **Fractal Courage Collective.** A guided 90-day coaching experience designed to support your transformation alongside the workbook. Every two weeks, join Renee and guest speakers for a 60-90 minute call where you:

- Deepen your workbook practice
- Build accountability and momentum
- Learn tools for self-regulation, creativity, and pattern interruption
- Connect with others on the same journey

This is not therapy. It is structured support, community insight, and steady encouragement.

Scan to Learn More
or Visit
fractalcourage.com

You can begin right where you are — and we will walk with you.

Acknowledgments

To my **test reader group**, thank you for lending your time, feedback, and encouragement as this project came to life. Your insights helped shape these pages into something honest and whole. I am deeply grateful for the way you showed up and believed in this vision from the beginning.

To **Michelle Gruening**, your mentorship, coaching, and relentless dedication helped pull me out of my perfection loop and into completion. You refused to let me hide behind "almost ready." Because of you, this book found its way into the world before Thanksgiving, in just about 120 days. Thank you for pushing me to get this story, and my journey, onto paper.

To all the **women in my life** who have befriended me, supported me, and stood beside me in my darkest moments, I am humbled to be counted among you. There are too many to name, but your love and resilience live between every line of this book.

To my sons, **Sam and Ben**, thank you for being my reason to keep showing up. Your light is my compass, your laughter my restoration.

To my sister, **Kathy**, your strength and loyalty have carried me through the hardest seasons. You are my safe harbor and my reminder that unconditional love is real.

To the **friends** who sat beside me in the dark without needing to fix the light, thank you. You taught me that healing begins in quiet companionship, not correction.

To the **mentors and teachers** whose wisdom helped me name my patterns and build new ones, your guidance reshaped my life and gave me the courage to begin again.

To **Anthony Gagliardo of Icarus Counseling**, thank you for your direction, support, and compassion. Your approach to counseling was nothing short of transformational, offering clarity and strength when I needed it most.

To my **Canvas Collective** and **Fractal Courage** communities, your willingness to tell the truth about your own stories inspired me to tell mine. You are living proof that restoration is possible, one micro act at a time.

And to **you, the reader,** thank you for walking this path with me. I see your bravery. I feel your heart. May you always find your way back to yourself.

About The Author

Renee King is an award-winning interior designer, author, and mentor who has spent more than two decades shaping environments that support beauty and emotional well-being. She built a career designing hospitality, entertainment, and behavioral health spaces, after first daring to launch her own firm in 2011 when the economy was still wobbling from the Great Recession.

Her deepest transformation, however, did not happen in a studio. It happened during a season of collapse that forced her to pause, turn inward, and rebuild from the ground up. What began as a 23-day sabbatical became the foundation for Fractal Courage, a framework built from small acts of honesty, creativity, and restoration.

***Fractal Courage: 23 Days to Me*™** offers readers the same path Renee used to climb out of survival mode and into a life shaped by truth. Her approach blends creative practice with pattern awareness, helping people see the loops that shape their lives, learn how to break them with intention, and strengthen their emotional resilience.

Today Renee leads workshops, creative healing sessions, group coaching experiences, and speaks to audiences about creative resilience, emotional restoration, and the power of pattern awareness. Her sessions blend reflective practice with art-based tools and journaling. She collaborates with guest speakers, wellness practitioners, and behavioral health professionals to create spaces where people can safely explore recovery, nervous system regulation, and the courage to return to themselves.

With years of experience in creative leadership and business strategy, Renee also teaches organizations how Fractal Courage principles apply to the workplace. Her work helps teams identify harmful patterns, reduce burnout, strengthen communication, and rebuild culture through clarity, consistency, and truth.

Renee plans to expand the Fractal Courage ecosystem into retreats, live workshops, and global offerings that support healing, creativity, and personal reinvention. Her commitment is simple and personal: to help others who feel lost or cracked open find a path back to themselves.

Renee lives in Liberty Lake, Washington, and is the mother of two sons who remain her greatest teachers and her steady source of joy. She continues to write, create, mentor, and build the movement that emerged from her own journey through the gap.

Learn more at www.fractalcourage.com

Made in the USA
Coppell, TX
29 January 2026

70242129R00056